John Chasteen

COACHING THE NEXT GENERATION

52 Ways
to Unleash
God-Given
Potential

TIMOTHY
Publishing Services

Coaching the Next Generation
© 2013 by John Chasteen

Published by Timothy Publishing Services
3409 W Gary St
Broken Arrow, OK 74012
918-924-6246

Unless otherwise noted, all Scripture quotations are taken from the Holy Bible, New International Version®, NIV®, © 1973, 1978, 1984 by International Bible Society. Used by permission of Zondervan Publishing House. All rights reserved worldwide.

Scripture quotations marked KJV are taken from the Holy Bible: King James Version.

Scripture quotations marked Amplified Bible are taken from The Amplified Bible, Old Testament, © 1965, 1987 by Zondervan Corporation. New Testament, © 1958, 1987 by The Lockman Foundation. Used by permission.

Where appropriate, the author has used the generic pronoun "he" to refer to either gender.

Copyediting: Shirley G. Spencer

ISBN: 978-1-940931-00-5

Library of Congress catalog card number: 2013954715

Printed in the United States of America

Endorsements

Coaching is the next step in leadership development. Most of us have mentors, guides, and spiritual fathers, but something more is needed. Coaching provides the platform for integrating all we received from earlier influencers. A good coach enables us to synthesize this formative training and bring out "things new," as Jesus instructed. John Chasteen coaches us well in this insightful book!

—Dr. A.D. Beacham, Jr., General Superintendent
International Pentecostal Holiness Church

I am a child of the church: born and reared in a pastor's home, graduating from Bible College, and seminary. I have pastored, served as the president of a Christian university, and am now a consultant with some of the largest churches in the world. One thing I have come to realize is that we are trying to meet needs without the appropriate tools in our possession. John Chasteen changes all that in *Coaching the Next Generation*. In a simple-to-follow, easy-to-implement format, John coaches us as we coach others. The church will be stronger because of *Coaching the Next Generation* by John Chasteen.

—Dr. Samuel R. Chand, Author
Cracking Your Church's Culture Code
(www.samchand.com)

A thorough, insightful and timely book, *Coaching the Next Generation,* will equip you to help others discover their potential. Whether you're a pastor or a born leader, this book will prove to be a valuable resource in your library.

—Craig Groeschel, Senior Pastor and Author
LifeChurch.TV, Edmond, Oklahoma

John Chasteen's *Coaching the Next Generation* is an exceptional read. I have been waiting for this book for a long time. This book helps mentors, life coaches, and spiritual fathers and mothers become effective in coaching their spiritual sons and daughters to recognize their full potential. *Coaching the Next Generation* is a biblically-based toolkit filled with practical field-tested insights on life coaching, listening, and empowering that can be implemented immediately.

John has been both a friend and life coach to me, and he has helped me understand my God-given potential and take steps to fulfill God's call on my life by using these principles. I highly recommend to you John's new book, *Coaching the Next Generation.*

—Larry Kreider, International Director
DOVE Christian Fellowship International
and author of over 30 books
including, *Authentic Spiritual Mentoring*

John's thought-provoking book is a powerful contribution to one's search for significance. Sadly, only about 30 percent of leaders finish well and leave a positive legacy. This percentage can be greatly increased by embracing the daily encouragements found in these pages. Chasteen is not only a coach; he is a practitioner of these principles. His recommendations for your journey come from life experience. I highly recommend this new book to all.

—Dr. Garnet E. Pike, President
SpiritLife Ministries, Oklahoma City

John Chasteen is an amazing author, coach and friend. There is something warm and encouraging about the way he communicates. Every time we are together, I come away inspired. His new book, *Coaching the Next Generation,* is a perfect mix of the wonderful insights and motivating thoughts I get to experience through our personal time together. If you are looking for a life-changing book that is easy to ready, this one is for you. I highly recommend *Coaching the Next Generation.*

—Dan Roberts, Entrepreneur, CEO
Trak-1 Technology

In this day and age, God is clearly renewing the hearts of men and women toward spiritual parenting. Now it is our responsibility to steward how we communicate that heart. Professional Coach Trainer Dr. John Chasteen has been doing that effectively for years and now you are about to enjoy the essence of what he has learned in the process.

I have no doubt that this book will help you maximize transformational connections and at the same time minimize transactional disconnects that would sabotage your calling to these emerging leaders.

—Dr. Joseph Umidi, Founder
Lifeforming Leadership Coaching

I am certain of Dr. John Chasteen's commitment to developing successful coaches. In years past, I have had the privilege of instructing John as a professor; now, he has taught me. I have personally seen his lectures open the eyes of pastors and leaders to the practicality and necessity of Christian coaching. John has an easy, practical way of getting his point across and his passion for coaching ignites a desire in his audience to embrace the coaching paradigm. Thank you, John, for your new book, *Coaching the Next Generation.*

—Dr. Owen Weston, DMin, PhD, President
CPR Institution and Coordinator of Doctoral Studies

Dedication

This book is dedicated to my amazing wife, Becky, the love of my life and my best friend. I dedicate it to her on behalf of her selfless and untiring support throughout the years.

Also to our three wonderful children Amy, Andrew, and Jon of whom we are so very proud.

To our awesome son-in-law, Charlie, who is such a blessing, along with our two daughters in-law Michele and Nicki, without whom we would be incomplete.

And finally, I dedicate this book to Chas, Karli, Corey, Maverick, and Jace, our five magnificent grandchildren who have brought us much joy.

Contents

Foreword   11

Acknowledgements   13

Introduction   15

PART I — UNDERSTANDING LIFE PURPOSE
  1 The Greatest Challenge on Earth   23
  2 You've Got Potential   25
  3 First Cousins Meet   27
  4 Walking the Road to Destiny   29
  5 Seeing What God Sees   33
  6 Discovering Life Purpose-I   35
  7 Discovering Life Purpose-II   39
  8 Find Uniqueness, Find Potential   41
  9 Now You See it, Now You Don't   43

PART II — THE POWER OF MEANINGFUL RELATIONSHIPS
  10 Having Great People in Your Life   47
  11 Get Real!   51
  12 Being First in the Vulnerability Line   53
  13 But I Don't Know You That Well   55
  14 How Much Will That Cost Me?   57
  15 When It's Gone, It's Gone   59

PART III — THE LOST ART OF LISTENING
  16 One Size Doesn't Fit All   65
  17 Can You Hear Me Now?   69
  18 Is Anybody Out There Listening?   71
  19 Reading Between the Lines   75
  20 Have You Crossed the Road Yet?   77
  21 I Don't Think They Get It!   79
  22 Getting Inside the Mind of Your Client   81
  23 Coaching With Empty Hands   83

PART IV — ASKING POWERFUL QUESTIONS
24 Questioning the Process   87
25 The "Columbo" Factor   89
26 Opening the Door But Not Leading the Way   93
27 Helping The Client With the Forensic Work   95
28 What Did You Mean by That?   97
29 The Flipside of Feedback   99
30 Questioning from a Non-judgmental Stance   101
31 Getting One's Head on Straight   103
32 Following Your Curiosity   105

PART V — KNOW THYSELF
33 How Did I Know That?   109
34 Interior Landscaping   113
35 Self-Consciousness Versus Self-Awareness   115
36 The Art of Extracting Lessons From Life   119
37 Searching for God Clues   121

PART VI — COACHING THROUGH THE HARD SPOTS
38 Chiseling God's Masterpieces   125
39 Mining the Metal   127
40 Turning Up the Heat   129
41 It is a Journey, Not an Event   131
42 Taking the Long Way Home   133
43 Engaging the Issues At Hand   135
44 Would You Hold Me Accountable?   137
45 Stretching the Mold   139

PART VII — VARIOUS AND SUNDRY ITEMS OF IMPORTANCE
46 Live So Nothing Is Wasted   145
47 Coming Out of Your Shell–Part I   147
48 Coming Out of Your Shell–Part II   151
49 Coming Out of Your Shell–Part III   155
50 Reframing Failure   157
51 Unhurried Time   159
52 Learning the Spiritual Coaching Stance   161

Conclusion   165

FOREWORD

I wasn't built for football, and I was too clumsy for basketball, so when I was growing up, I missed the experience of having a coach push me to my limits so I could help the team win a championship. But once I finished college, got married, and began my career, I realized that athletes aren't the only people who need coaches. If we are going to exceed in life, we need people to push us, encourage us, and—when necessary—blow the whistle on us.

When I met John Chasteen in 2003, we instantly bonded as friends. I saw all kinds of qualities in John that I wanted to emulate: he was wise, stable, decisive, compassionate, financially successful, and spiritually mature. He was a model husband, a good father, and skilled listener. Plus he was a few years older than I was, and he had a bit more gray hair than I had! I knew immediately that this was a guy I could look up to.

I began to refer to my new friend as "Coach John." He liked the nickname so much, in fact, that he started writing an article in a ministers' magazine that he titled "Hey, Coach John." My need for John's counsel and patient coaching actually pulled some new potential out of him as he developed his writing skills. Meanwhile, John has walked with me through some of the most difficult life transitions I've ever had to make. He has asked me hard questions, challenged my misconceptions, and helped me face my fears. Like any skilled coach, he saw potential in me that I didn't see in myself.

I spend a lot of time with ministers—some who are my age, and many who are younger. They often open up to me and say, "I don't have any close friends," or, "I really don't have any mentors or father figures in my life." My response is always the same: "How have you survived in ministry this long?" I don't believe God ever intended for us to live in isolation. We need healthy relationships—especially with older mentors who can offer encouragement, correction, and affirmation.

I'm blessed to have this kind of relationship with John Chasteen. I can call him for advice, lean on him for assurance, or ask him to call my bluff and kick me in the rear end. Everybody needs a relationship like that.

In this book, John makes it clear that a good coach is accessible and relational. If we are really going to unleash people's full potential—their talents and spiritual gifts—then we must care for them genuinely and invest in them consistently. John has done that for me, and I pray this book will help you do the same for many others.

How an athlete performs on the field is often determined by what a coach says in the locker room before the game. Encouragement is the key to success. This book is packed with encouragement that can help you win. In fact, each chapter is like a coach's pre-game pep talk. I pray John Chasteen's words will help unleash your full potential, and then equip you to be a skilled coach who can invest in the emerging generation.

— J. Lee Grady
Author and Christian activist
Contributing Editor Charisma Magazine

ACKNOWLEDGEMENTS

I would like to give credit that is due to Dr. Bobby Clinton of Fuller Theological Seminary. I had the awesome privilege of sitting under his life-changing teaching during my tenure at Southwestern Christian University. Four times to be exact! I owe much of my understanding of spiritual formation to him and his untiring devotion to study the lives of biblical, historical, and contemporary leaders.

Thank you, Dr. Clinton, for your hard work and research. You have blessed many.

INTRODUCTION
The Quiet Coaching Revolution

Coach – isn't that a word used in association with athletic events? Not any more, at least according to Gary Collins.[1] The coaching movement is alive and well both in the church and the corporate landscape of America. As a matter of fact, many businesses and organizations are scrambling to catch up with the coaching wave, implementing it into the very core of their value systems and putting it into practice from the boardroom to the break room.

Not surprisingly, church leaders across America are also incorporating coaching into their training protocol. Contemporary church movements, as well as mainline denominations are exploring coaching methodologies in order to better undergird their pastors, leaders, and ministers for 21st century effectiveness.

In essence, a silent undercurrent of preparation is now emerging that will soon release an army of coaches into the body of Christ worldwide.

How will this paradigm shift shape the church? Will it really make a difference? Or is it just another passing trend? Some in the church believe the coaching movement is here to stay. I happen to be one of them.

It is unlikely the coaching movement will take the world by storm. But I would like to pose to you a thought-provoking question: Could it be God's choice to use coaching through what I call "the leaven principle"? That is, could the coaching method gradually become an influence, a quiet force, transforming culture one life at a time? Only God knows for sure, but I would not be surprised at all if it happens.

I suppose my question to you would be: Are you ready for the quiet revolution?

Playing to Your Potential

Without a doubt, Wayne Gretzky was the greatest player in the game of hockey. Born and raised in Brantford, Canada, Gretzky started skating when he was two years old, and by the age of six, he was playing with boys several years older than he.

Gretzky played his way through school and became a professional hockey player in 1978. During his illustrious career, he played for several teams, including the Racers, Oilers, Kings, and Blues. He was inducted into the Hockey Hall of Fame in 1999. He is considered one of the best hockey players of all time, breaking numerous records. When asked once by a news reporter what made him so great, Gretzky replied, "While everyone else skated to where the puck was, I skated to where I thought it was going."[2]

Playing to potential is the key. It differentiates between leaders and followers, winners and losers. It is fundamental in achieving Bible-based success.

Understanding that everyone has God-given potential is paramount.

Although God-given potential is not a commodity to be compared among ourselves, it is crucial to walking in, and fulfilling, one's destiny. The notion that each of us has his own measure of God-given potential levels the playing field and gives every person the chance to succeed in his or her own right. Where you are headed (toward your potential) is possibly more important than where you have been.

Since moving toward your God-given potential is so important, may I contend that the greatest challenge for all humans on the planet is the question, "Who am I?" or "What is my God-given potential?"

As a spiritual father and coach, your clear assignment will be to help your sons and daughters face that very challenge. It's about helping them maximize their God-given potential and fulfill their life purpose and destiny.

It's not merely about rubber-stamping yourself on others (although what God has given you should be passed on in the form of mentoring and teaching). It's about shaping and molding others according to their God-given bent and helping them reach the measure God has put in them.

We are moving into an age when people have no desire to be just another carbon copy. Our culture has spawned a generation that demands authenticity and originality because most believe they are unique and have something to offer that no one else can give. Wow, what a thought!

Without a doubt, the concept of authenticity and originality is biblical; however, it becomes corrupted when God is left out of the equation. Pride, egotism, and conceit enter in and distort what God has put in the heart of each individual. Only with the help of the Christ, as the author and developer of our faith can an individual be perfectly cultivated to reach his potential (see Hebrews 12: 2).

As life coaches, we are co-laborers together with God. We are extensions of the ministry of the Holy Spirit. This happens as we come alongside people and draw out of them what God has put in them. As a skilled, trained, and anointed coach, you can help others reach their God-given potential.

Where do I start?

What is the starting point for moving members of the next generation toward their God-given potential? How do I motivate them to the point of change and help them become all God created them to be? That, my friend, is what this book is all about. My mission in writing the book is to address new models of learning and training that focus on

Christ-centered coaching and thus address the fatherlessness that plagues our land.

Addressing Our *Fatherlessness*

I believe we are living in the days of pronounced "fatherlessness" in the body of Christ.

It began as fallout from the Industrial Age when we subtly moved away from the apprentice concept of life and society. Unfortunately the Information Age has not faired any better but has moved us deeper into the hole, spawning what I call "an impersonal discipleship model" in the church. We've replaced one-on-one human interaction with mere information and called it discipleship. Now I'll be the first to tell you we need biblical information, yet not at the expense of human interaction. We need both working together. The result of our error from biblical discipleship has been an increase in fatherlessness in both the society and the church.

This malady has also opened wide the door for wolves dressed in sheep's clothing to enter. Charlatans, posing as leaders, have tampered with what the Spirit of God wants to do in this generation. For these and other reasons, the body of Christ is ready for a fresh understanding and a genuine renewal of spiritual fathers in the land; fathers who will coach, mentor, and disciple the upcoming generations.

I pray that God initiates a silent coaching revolution in the body of Christ. Could it be that a silent undercurrent of preparation is now evolving that eventually will release an army of coaches into action on a worldwide scale? I believe it is possible.

The Differentiation

As you read the book, you will notice a different paradigm subtly emerging, a method centered on the coaching paradigm. This example, simply put, is a more exploratory type of learning model in which the person being coached discovers truth. It stands somewhat in contrast to a traditional model of telling the person every move to make. I did this purposely to introduce you to the coaching model of discipleship and help you to see the biblical validity of the model.

The Layout

As you work your way through the material, you will notice that the layout of the book is also different. First, it is designed to be an easy read. You will not find a lot of eloquent language thrown in to impress you, nor will you be wading through academic verbiage that must be deciphered and ingested in order to get some "coded" message or meaning. Instead you will find a book that is clearly written and easy to follow.

Also, take note that the book can be read in sequence, that is, chapter by chapter, or simply at random. Each chapter is a lesson in itself. So whether you read systematically or sporadically peruse, the message is clear.

The book is divided into seven major divisions, each one representing a major coaching skill. In the midst of the seven divisions, 52 chapters unfold, each with a pithy title followed by a quote. A page or two follows with concisely worded advice, teaching, and instruction. Some chapters are short and to the point, others more lengthy. Each chapter will help you get a handle on what potential looks like in real life and how to draw it out.

Keep in mind the book is not meant to be an in-depth teaching on the subject of coaching; however, it is designed to create an appetite in you to learn more about the coaching paradigm or model. Equally important is my desire to evoke in you a pursuit for God-given potential and learn to "think biblically" in fresh ways, or, as some would term, "outside the box."

Finally, I want to drive home the importance of discovering your God-given potential. I love the statement credited to

André Gide: "I'd rather fail at being myself than to succeed at being someone else." To me, that is the impetus for both discovering and helping others find their God-given potential.

Above all, put these ideas to use. Apply them to your life and your relationships with the next generation. Use them with your family around the supper table, but don't limit them only to that setting. Take them everywhere—from the boardroom to the break room. Let the silent coaching revolution begin!

PART I

UNDERSTANDING LIFE PURPOSE

"Do not go where the
path may lead, go instead
where there is no path
and leave a trail."
—Ralph Waldo Emerson

Life Purpose is a hot topic in today's world. Some believe it's trendy because our culture has created this veracious social vacuum that has left people feeling empty and lacking. That could be true. However, at a deeper level, the quest for life purpose is as old as mankind.

I believe life purpose and God-given potential are inextricably linked. So to understand the first is to realize the second. The measure of your potential is wrapped up in your life purpose. This is a liberating concept because it frees you from trying to be me and me from trying to be you.

In this section of the book I will endeavor to connect life purpose and God-given potential. I will also give you a biblical context and model for helping others discover their life purpose. The goal is to enable you to move others exponentially toward their God-given potential and the results will become apparent.

1

THE GREATEST CHALLENGE ON EARTH

Discovering God's Purpose For Your Life

↓

"... It's not about you."

—Rick Warren

Rick Warren opens his bestseller, The Purpose Drive Life, with the infamous words, "It's not about you."[3] He continues making his point by showing that it's really all about God. I believe that, don't you? It's all about God's purposes and how our lives fit into His master plan.

As powerful and true as these statements are, the oxymoron of the issue is this: although it's really not about you, it has to do with you. We are all on a journey to discover our destiny, sometimes known as our God-given purpose. The journey is long and often treacherous. Ironically at times purpose can be elusive, seemingly just out of reach. I believe it happens to be the greatest challenge on earth.

Who am I? What is my potential? These are the questions that motivate all mankind regardless of nationality, creed, race and socio-economic status. The human race is searching.

So all mankind is on a journey of discovery; a search, a mission to uncover what's been put within us—a discovery, if you will, and an excursion that begins somewhere in adolescence and continues until the day you die. It's important to know that it's a lifelong process.

It's a God-given quest. And the reason it takes a lifetime is that God has invested so much in you that you can't possibly discover it all at once; it would blow you away. So your God-given purpose is inseparably linked with your potential. To discover purpose, is to realize potential and that's why we coach.

In Ecclesiastes, Solomon wrote: "He has made everything beautiful in its time. He also has planted eternity in men's hearts and minds [a divinely implanted sense of a purpose working through the ages which nothing under the sun but God alone can satisfy], yet so that men cannot find out what God has done from the beginning to the end." (3:11, Amplified Bible).

He has set "a divinely-implanted sense of purpose" in your heart. That's the tug with which all humanity grapples. A call to be, and to do, to live out one's God-given potential. As a spiritual parent, do you know how to spot it in those you are coaching? How to release them to walk in it? That is the task at hand and the focus of this book.

2

YOU'VE GOT POTENTIAL

Man's Search for Meaning in Life

"If you had to identify, in one word, the reason why the human race has not achieved, and never will achieve, its full potential, that word would be 'meetings.'"

—Dave Barry

Have you ever heard the statement, "We're all here for a reason"? I can recall encounters with what the Bible would call wicked people who've readily admitted to me, "I know I'm here for a purpose, but I just don't know what it is." I have also known of individuals who've experienced a serious brush with death to say, "God must have a reason for keeping me around."

They are right. We are all here for a purpose.

According to Ecclesiastes 3:11 (Amplified Bible), every person has a "divinely implanted" sense of purpose. By purpose we are referring to a call, a sense of destiny. You might say it's an appointment with God and certain life experiences. The search for that life purpose is in essence the discovery of your God-given potential.

The search described above kicks in somewhere around adolescence. From there it becomes a lifelong quest. Think about it: how old was Jesus when He was left behind in Jerusalem as a youth and later found by His parents in the temple discussing spiritual matters with the scribes and lawyers? He was 12 years old. It seems this God-given search kicks into gear during the preteen and teen years. In our culture, we sometimes call it rebellion, and it might resemble it at times. Could it actually be something else? Might it be God initiating the search for His purpose planted in our lives?

During the teen years, an individual begins a relentless pursuit to discover who he is, where he fits in, and how he will accomplish the tasks set before him. These and other signs are all symptomatic of a God-ordained search.

I find it ironic that although the search begins in adolescence, most people are not aware of what is happening. Many don't have a clue and blame it on "growing pains," circumstances, or other outside issues (not meant to be a statement of unconcern for real emotional pain). I believe it is in essence the search for significance, the age-old quest for potential.

So, I say, "Let the search begin!" As a coach, you can accommodate the individual in his quest by using coaching techniques such as probing with powerful questions, listening intently, and affirming the person as he sifts through his experiences, often with frustration and uncertainty. You won't help him resolve it all; it's a life process that often requires years of process and work.

We will follow this thought more in the next chapter.

3

FIRST COUSINS MEET

The Intertwining of Destiny, Purpose and Potential

> "Definiteness of purpose is the starting point of all achievement."
> —W. Clement Stone

The word *destiny* has somewhat of a lofty sound, don't you think? It evokes the mysterious and is often tossed around in our dealings with future issues. But how much do you really know about destiny? For instance, what is the biblical explanation for the term? How does it link with life purpose? Or potential? Let's find out.

For starters, the term *destiny* is never mentioned in the Bible (KJV); however, the concept of destiny is interwoven throughout the pages of God's Word and is recognized as a gift from God.

Destiny is an old English word that literally means, "a future juncture."[4] The idea is that of an intersection; literally one's path intersecting with future events and happenings.

In biblical thinking, destiny is always linked with God. In simple terms, this means that somewhere in your future, God's path and yours will interconnect. When this occurs, destiny takes place.

It is important to understand that fate and destiny are opposites. Fate represents that which is out of your control. It implies that you become a puppet in the hand of some mindless power that makes illogical and coincidental things happen.

Destiny, on the other hand, refers to something that is predetermined by someone larger and more loving than you. Yet in a mysterious way, you play a role in it. You participate, by choice. See the difference?

I concur with many people who believe that destiny is often determined by design. In Genesis 1, we find God creating vast amounts of sky known as the heavens. When the time came to fill the heavens, He created inhabitants uniquely designed to fill that space, winged creatures designed to fulfill their destiny of moving in the heavens. The same holds true for every living creature in the biblical account. Each one was uniquely crafted for its particular destiny.

So by now you are probably asking yourself, could this also be true of mankind? Absolutely. God established a pattern in the book of beginnings that can be seen throughout time and eternity.

Helping others understanding their God-given design is essential. It plays a great role in grasping their God-ordained destiny. It is often easier to see design in others before we see it in ourselves. A skilled coach will direct the client toward this important area of growth. Does this mean God will never ask you to do anything that deviates from your design? Absolutely not. However, when one surrenders all he is, God can use his gifts, natural abilities, and skills as He chooses.

So here is what it might look like if you are coaching someone toward his God-given potential. Begin by asking some good questions: What is your passion? How are you wired? Have you given it all to God? Remember, God will use who you are, when he has all of you.

4

WALKING THE ROAD TO DESTINY

In Search of Our God-given Purpose

"Destiny is usually just around the corner. But what destiny does not do is home visits. You have to go for it."

—Carlos Ruiz Zafon

As alluded to in an earlier chapter, destiny is often seen by people as some sort of spooky, mystical experience designed for just a few of God's chosen people. We view it as something most of us common people don't have to worry about ever experiencing. It's as if only the elite get chosen for destiny.

But is that really a biblical view? I don't think so. As a matter of fact, every person living and breathing can expect a brush with destiny at some point in his life.

A study of Scripture reveals this as a relatively common experience for all who choose to follow God's path. Sooner or later, everyone runs face first into his destiny. The key is for individuals to learn to recognize destiny when it smacks them in the face, or to see what I call *signposts* along the way.

What are the road signs we tend to overlook? I like how Dr. Bobby Clinton discloses the path of destiny in his book, *Strategic Concepts That Clarify a Focused Life.*[5] He aptly describes destiny's voice, or the signposts, by using several terms to which we can relate: (1) a sense of destiny; (2) a destiny insight; (3) a destiny experience; and (4) destiny fulfilled.

1. A Sense of Destiny. God uses many different methods to impart a sense of destiny in a person. At times it is revelatory in nature. At other times, it can be a bit more speculative. Generally speaking, God will simply pull back the curtain of your life and show you something about your future. It can be a mystical moment, but it doesn't have to be. Regardless of the emotion felt, that spiritual experience becomes your sense of destiny. On the other side of the coin, some people have merely a growing sense of urgency or "knowing" that begins to permeate their lives and affect their view of the future.

2. Destiny Insight. Dr. Clinton categorizes this step as understanding or insight that is usually more supernatural in nature. A destiny insight is more than a hunch or a good idea (sense of destiny). It's beyond an aspiration or daydream. It's revelatory in nature, which puts it into a category of its own.

Joshua's famous twilight stroll on the eve of the Jericho invasion is a good example of gaining destiny insight. He encountered a heavenly visitor sent to fight as the captain of the Lord of Hosts. Do you think Joshua received helpful insight about the outcome of the battle slated for the next day? I think so.

3. Destiny-evoking experience. Although closely related to a sense of destiny, a destiny-evoking experience is a step beyond the previous occurrence. God will often give people experiences that are a strong indication of a future destiny.

It could be something like a brush with death in which your client was preserved or anything that speaks to him in a powerful way that God's blessing and calling is working in his life. These become strong indicators that show the person that God is involved in his life and a destiny lies ahead.

For the biblical patriarch Joseph, a series of explicit dreams instilled in him an indelible imprint of destiny. For John Wesley, it was a childhood fire. Against unbelievable odds, he was preserved in a life-threatening situation and it became his destiny experience. For the biblical leader Joshua, it was an encounter with an angel on the eve of the Jericho invasion.

What can you think of that might have been a destiny-evoking experience in your life?

4. Destiny Fulfilled. In coaching, our goal is to arouse that sense of destiny in the person and help him explore it. This sense of destiny is often buried beneath a mound of disappointment and heartache. It could have been put on the back burner due to prolonged delay or deferment. Whatever the case, it's your job to direct your spiritual son or daughter back on the trail again.

A key exercise in which to engage the next generation would be the simple art of reflection. This is often where a good coach will help his client revisit many of life's back roads things that may have been overlooked, clues that have been hidden and forgotten. Have those you are coaching keep a journal as they perform these exercises. You may be surprised at what surfaces and becomes associated with their destiny.

5

SEEING WHAT GOD SEES

Seeing Things From God's Perspective

"Let discernment be your trustee, and mistakes your teacher."

—T.F. Hodge

The art of helping others unleash their God-given potential is really all about helping them see what God sees in them. Sounds easy, right? It may appear to be an easy process, but it's not always so. This is why coaches are so necessary today.

Some of the most explicit examples of coaching spring from Scripture passages linked with Paul and his team of "fellow laborers." Probably one of the better known cases was a man named Barnabas. I call him a world-class "coach/mentor."

Few people recognize the interesting twist found in reference to Barnabas' name change. In Acts 4:36, Luke states that the apostles bestowed on him the name, Barnabas. The name itself gives valuable insight into the philosophy and mindset that Joseph (Barnabas) modeled and practiced to influence many in the early church. It also helps us understand biblical discipleship and how the coaching model dovetails with it, providing a good fit for today's society.

Ample evidence supports the fact that Joseph's new name, Barnabas, might have been given as an insight to his prophetic nature and gifting. That is the conclusion of F.F. Bruce in his highly respected commentary, *The Book of Acts*.[6] French Arrington, the revered Church of God scholar, comments on the same verse by saying that the name "Barnabas is Arabic and conceivably it means son of prophecy."[7] Both Bruce and Arrington acknowledge the possibility of his name being associated with a prophetic gift or bent in his temperament.

Simply said, Barnabas had an element in his gifting that allowed him to see potential in others. He saw what God saw in people. Remember his help with Saul, who later became Paul? What about John Mark and the insights Barnabas had into his potential? Was it accurate? Yes, Mark ended up writing one of the Gospels we read today. Did he see potential in others? Absolutely.

At times you and I will need the help of seasoned coaches to recognize the potential in our lives. The challenge and tests of life can dim the eye and darken the soul. When this happens, the arrow tends to veer off course.

Remember, potential can be elusive, hard to define, especially in our younger years. A good coach can help us focus and get back on track. Do you see potential in others? Have you confirmed that with them?

Every person needs a Barnabas in life, someone who sees potential in us and is not afraid to speak to it.

6

DISCOVERING LIFE PURPOSE-I

Finding Your God-given Passion

> "If you want to identify me, ask me not where I live, or what I like to eat, or how I comb my hair, but ask me what I am living for...."
>
> —Thomas Merton

A common thread through this first division in the book is the idea that discovering your Life Purpose (LP) is the equivalent of comprehending your God-given potential.

By LP I am referring to what gets you out of bed every morning, that one or two factors that make you work tirelessly; that "cause" you would follow even without financial remuneration, if necessary. Call it your North Star, your sweet spot, a stabilizer ... whatever. That is your life purpose and therein lies your God-given potential.

As powerful as LP is, it can be one of the most elusive things we deal with. We will address that topic in detail in another chapter, but the primary reason it is so elusive is because it is a lifelong pursuit, a discovery process, a journey, if you will.

Did you know that this journey is a God-given quest? Why do you suppose this is so? Here are several scriptural reasons why finding your God-given potential is a lifelong process.

"He has made everything beautiful in its time. He also has planted eternity in men's hearts and minds (a divinely implanted sense of purpose working through the ages which nothing under the sun but God alone can satisfy), yet so that men cannot find out what God has done from the beginning to the end." (Ecclesiastes 3:11, Amplified Bible)[8]

Notice several interesting details about this verse:

1. You have a divinely implanted sense of purpose.

This means you are always trying to discover who you are, where you are going, and other related issues. Interestingly, this quest for identity and sense of purpose usually kicks in about adolescence. How old was Jesus when He said, "I must be about my Father's business"?

2. It is a God-given search.

He has planted eternity in men's hearts. This means your life is linked with God's purposes. Notice where He put it in your heart. This means God has equipped you with spiritual DNA that links you with your purpose.

Many call DNA a natural phenomenon; I call it a supernatural wonder. Your natural DNA is like your thumbprint; unless you are an identical twin, no one else on the planet has exactly the same DNA as you. It is yours and yours alone.

In simple terms, your DNA is a molecular code that commands and programs every cell in your body. Actually the nucleus of every cell in your body has DNA stored within what is called chromosomes. Inside this string of commands lies your entire physical composition, including the color of your hair, your height, skin color, the shape of your nose, eyes, and ears. It also controls many other aspects of your life, including personality, behavior traits, and the list goes on.

If the instructions in the DNA were words and you typed them out, experts say it would be the equivalent of 200 phone books. That is in one cell. And we have trillions of cells in our bodies. Wow!

You also have a spiritual DNA, written in your heart. A coach can help pull that out of you. This is important, simply because one of the many signs of true spiritual maturity is when a person stops trying to be someone else, a carbon copy, and becomes an original.

Remember, it's a process. Do you know what's in your spiritual DNA?

7

DISCOVERING LIFE PURPOSE-II

Understanding Your Spiritual DNA

"What am I living for and what am I dying for are the same question."

—Margret Atwood

Since you and I have a unique spiritual DNA stored in our heart, it would stand to reason that it must be mined, brought forth, and developed. It is important to understand that this process takes much more than some humanistic formula. In essence, it is a work of God. Yes, we are co-laborers together with Him, but we must never forget that He is the author and finisher of our faith. It is not a work of man.

"He has made everything beautiful in its time. He also has planted eternity in men's hearts *and* minds [a divinely implanted sense of a purpose working through the ages which nothing under the sun but God alone can satisfy], yet so that men cannot find out what God has done from the beginning to the end." (Ecclesiastes 3:11, Amplified Bible)

In continuing our look at discovering life purpose, it is extremely important to see that the thread of life purpose runs through every generation. It is something God has been, and is still, involved with throughout every generation. Every person deals with it, regardless of his race, color, or ethnicity. It is manifested in every generation, from builders to X'ers and all in-between.

Is it any wonder our hearts are always searching? Is it any wonder we always sense there is more?

Could it be that what we feel is a divine stirring? Perhaps our hearts are restless because this divine call has been extended to each of us. I believe so.

Call it a longing, a search for significance, or whatever you like, but God alone can satisfy this divine longing. Money can't buy it; relationships are good, but they are no substitute. It takes an encounter with God to find real life purpose, because your purpose is wrapped up in Him.

It is expedient for you to understand that you don't know everything about your life purpose. It doesn't unfold suddenly. It's progressive in nature. It's not an A to Z happening; rather, it is revealed gradually, a process to be cherished and treasured. And here's the clincher: you have to walk it out to figure it out.

Who's helping you as you hit the trail? And who are you going to help in their journey?

Can you articulate your Life Purpose?

8

FIND UNIQUENESS, FIND POTENTIAL

Becoming Who God Made You To Be

> *"You are unique; when God created you He broke the mold and said, 'I'll never do that again!'"*
> —Bishop Tony Miller

Typically, individual uniqueness has not been a valued commodity in most evangelical circles. Instead, we've majored on reproducing ourselves. The end result has been the "rubber-stamping" of too many Christians and the squelching of God-given potential.

I realize this is a strong statement, so at this point it might be good to insert a disclaimer. I'm not saying that passing on our expertise and experience is a bad thing; however, to honor individual uniqueness is to glorify the magnificence and endless creativity of God.

To observe uniqueness is to realize a person's potential. Hence, the coach must learn early on to develop an eye for the potential that often lies latent within the person. In order to do this, you must learn to do as Susan Scott states in her book,

Fierce Conversations: "Come into the conversation with empty hands. Bring nothing but yourself."[9]

The starting point for spotting potential is recognizing that all people are unique by God's design. As a human being, it's easy to compare one person to another. As a coach, you must squelch that tendency. If you don't, you will find yourself interpreting the person rather than really understanding him. To interpret someone is to categorize him or her into a mental or cultural pigeonhole.

These types of classifications are generally based on your past experience with other people. It's the idea of, "Oh, I've dealt with your kind before. You are...." When this happens, you stop listening and start misunderstanding people. When you pigeonhole people, you practice disrespect and become, instead, a respecter of persons, which is something God warns us against in James 2:1-4.

Could this be what Jesus meant when He gave serious counsel about being over judgmental (Matthew 7:1-2)?

Ask yourself the question Susan Scott asks her clients: "Would I rather be understood or interpreted?"[10] Most of us would rather be heard and understood. Right? If that's the case, then please afford others the same privilege you would give yourself.

So the coach must see every client as a unique individual created by God and learn to resist the allurement of "interpreting people." When you do, you will begin to see and appreciate the uniqueness of each person. This is the starting point of spotting potential.

Author's Note: (I am not referring to individual uniqueness as an excuse for fleshly behavior and sin.)

9

NOW YOU SEE IT, NOW YOU DON'T

The Elusiveness of Potential

"Thinking something does not make it true. Wanting something does not make it real."

—Michele Hodkin

The disposition of potential is often one of elusiveness. That which should be easy to spot has a way of becoming difficult to bring to light. It is like the proverbial "carrot on a stick" that always seems to be just out of reach. There are several reasons for this elusiveness, but primarily it is due to the fact that undeveloped potential can be implicit and unclear. It is often sketchy and hard to articulate at best, especially in the younger person or leader.

The individual being coached has to learn to meet the elusiveness of potential head-on in order to conquer it. As a coach, you're responsible to facilitate him in this area. The coach must evoke a hunger in the client to know more about God as well as his own potential, and he must become intentional about finding it. No one ever coincidentally bumps into potential, since it rarely comes looking for you.

So where does one start looking for that elusive element of God-given potential? I believe there are many places to begin, but one starting point is simply learning to extract experiences and lessons from one's own life.

Here are a few suggestions to help:

1. Practice the art of reflection.

In the Scriptures we find the term *reflection* referred to as *meditation*. The Hebraic word means to "mutter to oneself." The connotation is to practice repeatedly, to contemplate, reflect, and distill the lessons at hand.

The problem is that most of us seldom slow down long enough for serious reflection. God also encourages us recurrently in Scripture to remember. The Passover Feast celebrated annually was simply a remembrance of the Israelites' deliverance from Egyptian slavery.

To remember is to reflect.

2. Pay attention to your passion.

I like to draw people's attention to what I call their passion radar that which causes the client to light up when he thinks about it. It could be defined as his "sweet spot" or "gifted area of life." So this means having him perform several assignments, paying close attention to what feels right and proper for his particular spiritual giftedness.

So the search for God-given potential can feel much like, "Now you see it, now you don't." At times we feel we are consumed with it; at other time, we seem sidetracked. It can almost seem as though God is hiding it from us or keeping us in the dark in some way. The fact is, life purpose and potential are not always easy to grasp. One reason might be the fact that whatever one purchases becomes his treasure.

If grasping and fulfilling life purpose were easy, everybody would be doing it. But not everybody is on that quest. Are You? The tell-tale sign of progress is moving life purpose from an ideation (thought; idea) to articulation.

PART II

THE POWER OF MEANINGFUL RELATIONSHIPS

"The meeting of two personalities is like the contact of two chemical substances: if there is any reaction, both are transformed."

—C.G. Jung

God's desire is not that you and I walk through life alone. No, he has preplanned that you connect with others whom He will use to shape and prepare you for your destiny. Therefore, meaningful relationships are a must when it comes to unleashing our God-given potential.

You will never become all God intended you to be without significant people in your life. You've heard the saying, "If you find a turtle on a fencepost, you know he didn't get up there by himself." It's true! We always stand on the shoulders of others.

This section of the book will introduce the building blocks of meaningful relationships. You will also gain insight into the importance of connecting with your spiritual sons and daughters, and exactly how to do it.

10

HAVING GREAT PEOPLE IN YOUR LIFE

The Power of Significant People in Our Lives

"The older I grow,
the more I am convinced that
there is no education which one can
get from books and costly apparatus
that is equal to that which
can be gotten from contact
with great men and women."

—Booker T. Washington

Over the years, I have noticed a powerful principle that seems to run true in the lives of all great leaders. It's simple, yet profound: every great leader has significant people in his or her life.

Leadership guru J. Robert Clinton says, "Major development takes place in the life of a leader through significant people whom God brings into their path at crucial times."[11] With that in mind, significant people are indispensable and absolutely necessary.

As you are coaching individuals to reach their God-given potential, you will often find people who have skirted this important principle. Yet, everybody needs someone they look up to and connect with. Although coaching and mentoring are somewhat different paradigms, the importance of significant people in our lives is a transferrable model. Dr. Clinton suggests several things to help us find those significant people:[12]

1. The Law of Attraction

The starting point for connecting with significant people is attraction. This usually begins with a strong inner desire to imitate or emulate another person's life or ministry.

This is often a God-given attraction.

2. The Bond of Relationship

From attraction grows a bond of trust that turns into a relationship. Relationship refers to a growing interactive trust between you and significant people, which is the basis of response and accountability.

You and I should never take our relationships for granted; rather, we should work diligently at maintaining them.

3. Reciprocating Responsiveness

In your relationships with significant people, you must respond to their input. This simply means submission. People of substance don't have time to waste; only by response will you catch their ear.

If you and I are not willing to respond to important people, we will never get the sharpening we need.

4. Practicing Accountability

Significant people are often identified by the way they exercise accountability. Leaders always hold others accountable; however, they too are accountable to their peers and superiors.

If accountability is missing in your relationships, you will receive very little from them.

5. Practicing Empowerment

A clear sign of leadership is the person's ability to empower others. Empowerment is the act of enablement. Leaders will not bind you to themselves; rather, they will empower you to succeed and follow God's will for your life and ministry.

You and I will never become all God wants us to be without significant people in our lives. So the question each of us needs to answer is "Who do I have in my life? Who is my hero? With whom do I connect, and who is connecting with me?" There is where you will find the significant people you need in your journey toward destiny.

You are a product of the great people in your life.

11

GET REAL!

Learning to Be Transparent

"Sunlight is the best disinfectant."
—William O. Douglas

The body of Christ in America is suffering from a lack of biblical authenticity. By authenticity I am referring to the character trait that denotes transparency, openness, and, yes, at times even vulnerability. By definition, it's an unusual willingness to share one's inner life with others. Not surprisingly, transparency is glaringly lacking in most American relationships. Call it pride or just "rugged individualism," whatever it is, it severely hinders meaningful relationships.

I have a hunch that the reason for this lack of transparency could be a form of reactionary response to the fall of so many major leaders over the last 30 years. An inordinate amount of leaders who had become household names in that era fell from grace not to mention the thousands of nameless pastors and leaders. (I say that with great sorrow and regret.)

The fallout from this dilemma has produced a clandestine church as congregations have slowly become hush-hush, private, if you will. Many churches have lost their transparency, so much so that it is difficult to even have a good altar service in many places. People are no longer willing to share their struggles and weaknesses for fear of being ostracized. The result of this weakness is that we sit arm in arm with hurting people, often never even realizing it. We've created a culture of silence that makes it taboo to catalyze authenticity.

So how does this affect the discovery of one's God-given potential? Whether we like it or not, much of our discovery of potential comes through visiting the painful areas of our lives. This includes examining our own failures and shortcomings. By working through these sensitive areas, insight arises. Often the process is healing and medicinal, freeing us from the past.

As coaches, we must learn to personally catalyze authenticity and promote it in our relationships. Here are a few tips for doing that:

1. Be willing to share your inner life with the person you're coaching.

Modeling biblical authenticity does not mean pulling all your skeletons out of the closet and sharing every problem you've ever had. Rather, it means being willing to simply share your inner life with the one you are coaching. Develop a willingness to talk about real life issues, possibly a weakness or a shortcoming, not being afraid to start the conversation.

2. Learn that failing does not make you a failure.

In the Bible, God pulls no punches. Regardless of who the person is or who he is perceived to be, the Bible readily exposes his faults and struggles, and, I might add, without reluctance. Why? So we can understand how bad people really are? No, but there are several legitimate reasons, like exposing sin and wickedness and helping us understand the principle of biblical authenticity.

It is easy as a coach to leave the impression that you've never struggled with anything. When this happens, it may cause your client to put a wall between him and you and to feel as though he is unworthy because he has so many issues.

The bottom line is that it is okay to talk about past disappointments, discouragements, and struggles. Go ahead; share a war story or two. The younger generation of ministers and emerging leaders need to hear them. Just do not leave it in the valley; share how God brought you through.

The question is, "Are you secure enough to tell yours?"

12

BEING FIRST IN THE VULNERABILITY LINE

Catalyzing Authenticity

↓

"Honesty is the first chapter of the book wisdom."

—Thomas Jefferson

The word *catalyze*, in its simplest form, means to start or initiate an action, to influence.[11] It carries the idea of one being the match that strikes the fire, the original hotspot, a change agent, if you please. As coaches, we must learn to be catalysts for authenticity with our clients. We can't wait for them to lead the way. We must not only talk about transparency, we must learn to demonstrate it.

In Scripture, we find that God often uses authenticity to eliminate barriers in relationships sometimes quickly, I might add. I Corinthians 1:27 says, "God uses the weak things of the world to confound the mighty."

Transparency often cuts through all the red tape that accumulates in relationships. It disarms defenses and unmasks the weaknesses that humanity keeps in the shadows. When a client experiences authenticity from his coach, he is freed to be real, to take off his mask. The result is a relationship built on openness and transparency. Do you catalyze authenticity, or do you play it safe?

A simple way to do this in conversation is to share your greatest victory along with your greatest challenge. Your greatest victory will come easy; however, pulling back the curtain of your heart and bearing your challenge may be difficult.

When sharing your greatest challenge, consider the following pointers to help catalyze authenticity in the hearer:

1. Share your story using personal emotions.

Displaying personal emotions makes the story real. Words such as, *I felt like...*, or *my hopes sank...* draw people into the drama of your challenge. It helps them realize that you are not some protected person isolated from the battlefield.

Don't be afraid to express emotions.

2. Don't drag out your story too long.

If you wallow in your sorrows for 15 minutes, your client will have moved from empathy to impatience. Watch your time when sharing your challenge. Also, change the focus from your valley experience, to how you over came and made it a mountain-top experience.

3. Always conclude your story on a high note.

Never leave the story in the valley. Make it victorious, a story of overcoming. If you are still in process with the story, keep it positive and couched in faith and trust in God.

How authentic are you? Do you share your inner life with others? Are you transparent about your personal struggles, frustrations, and challenges? Perhaps today is a good time to start.

Keep in mind that authenticity is a must for your clients' discovery of their God-given potential. Many treasures lie in the ruins of their lives the areas they are too embarrassed to revisit. Your authenticity will help.

(Author's note: I do not advocate sharing private concerns with one's clients. I do believe a person should use wisdom and share appropriately with others. A good rule of thumb is that if you are still challenged in an area, share it only with your superiors.)

13

BUT I DON'T KNOW YOU THAT WELL

The Power of Connection With Others

"In the past a leader was a boss. Today's leaders must be partners with their people... they no longer can lead solely based on positional power."

—Ken Blanchard

Potential is realized frequently through the power of meaningful relationships. It is often called forth and nurtured by those around us. If that is the case, then it begs the question: "Am I connected with individuals who can sharpen me?"

The Scripture teaches this principle: "As iron sharpens iron, so one person sharpens another" (Proverbs 27:17). Notice the passage did not say paper hones iron, or wood refines iron. No, it takes iron to sharpen iron. Strength begets strength, and for that reason, you need strong people in your life.

Here are a few tips concerning how you can connect with the right people in your life.

1. All great people have great people in their lives.

For Moses, it was Jethro; for Joshua, it was Moses. So we see a principle in place that states, "In order for you to practice greatness, you need to surround yourself with great people." You need the influence and wisdom of a person who has gone farther down the road than you; someone who has "been there and done that," and can help you as you mature in life.

2. It takes someone stronger than you to sharpen you.

You will never mature beyond the level of strength found in your closest relationships. With that in mind, who do you have that is a "10" on the maturity scale?

3. Promotion generally comes through relationship.

Joshua's promotion came because he walked with Moses; Elisha walked with Elijah; and Timothy followed Paul. Looking for promotion? Look for God-given relationships with great people.

Those who isolate themselves weaken their highest potential. It took Barnabas's prophetic gift to recognize Paul's greatness; it was Jesus who called forth the "rock" qualities in Peter. Who is calling forth that God-given potential in you?

"I don't know you that well" is no excuse for not having meaningful relationships in your life.

14

HOW MUCH WILL THAT COST ME?

Building and Spending Relational Capital

"Life is an awful, ugly place to not have a best friend."
—Sarah Dessen

In the world of friends and friendships, building and establishing relational capital is imperative. Relational capital is a metaphoric term used to explain the idea that our relationships resemble a bank account. Whether we realize it or not, you and I are constantly making deposits and withdrawals by virtue of our everyday interactions in life. In the social world, relational capital and trust are synonymous.

All relationships are built on trust. In order to maintain a reasonable level of capital, deposits and withdrawals must be kept in balance. A coaching relationship also requires this type of ongoing give and take. It is almost as if a tension must be balanced in order to keep the relationship from fracturing. The balance is accomplished by the coach being intentional about depositing into the relationship on a regular basis. This is done in a variety of ways but primarily through the use of words, actions, and attitudes.

Consider the following examples:
- Sacrificing for a person or a friendship
- Meeting or exceeding expectations
- Gentleness
- Timeliness when it's called for
- Keeping your word
- Supporting someone in time of need
- Acts of kindness—valentines, cards, flowers, notes
- Praise or affirmation
- Encouragement
- Trusting a person in important matters
- Believing in a person, naming his or her gifts, calling things out of him or her
- Believing the best about someone
- Exercising positive influence
- Acceptance
- Apologizing, admitting your mistakes and misdeeds[14]

As insignificant as these points may seem, they are foundational in all relationships. Most breakdowns in relationships are centered on one or several of these areas. The stronger the relationship, the deeper the trust. The deeper the trust, the more explicit the transformation.

Are you building relational capital in those you are coaching? Are you intentional about it?

Fulfilling potential is really about change.

15

WHEN IT'S GONE, IT'S GONE

Spending Your Relational Capital Wisely

"Never leave a friend behind.
Friends are all we have to get us
through this life—and they are the
only things from this world that we
could hope to see in the next."
—Dean Koontz

As my brother and I were growing up, our mother would give us a whopping allowance of $2 per week. Momma always told us, "You had better spend your allowance wisely, because when it's gone, it's gone."

The same is true with your relational capital. Once you've overdrawn your account, the likelihood of reconnecting with the person is slim to none, or at least until more deposits are made. Proverbs puts it this way: "A brother offended is harder to win than a fortified city." (Prov. 18:19, KJV)

So here is the question that implores an answer: "Why is the issue of relational capital such an important focal point in coaching the next generation?"

The primary reason is that as a coach, you are endeavoring to pull important information out of your clients; to bring them face to face with their constraints, that one issue everybody else sees, but they can't. Often it has to do with pride or fear. In some individuals, it might be a matter of incompetence. Whatever it is, it's usually painful and deeply ingrained within them.

If you happen to wound your client deeply, it's over. The offended rarely open up. For these and other reasons, you have to spend your relational capital wisely.

So how do we exercise caution in spending our relational capital with the person we are coaching? And how do you recognize when an emotional withdrawal has happened? Here are a few examples of actions that can deplete your relational capital:

- Intentionally or even unintentionally exploiting another person
- Thinking of yourself first
- Treating a person or friendship as trivial
- Failing to meet clear expectations of the other person
- Harshness
- Inconveniencing another through lateness
- Breaking your word
- Not being there emotionally or by simply ignoring a need
- Forgetting important dates or remembrances
- Making fun of or denigrating a person
- Belittlement of discouraging situations
- Distrusting a person
- Not believing in a person, seeing him or her as unnecessary or beneath you
- Exercising power or manipulation
- Refusing to apologize, blaming others[15]

By examining this list, you may see some areas in which you have spent your relational capital unwisely. Circle the ones that need work. Become intentional concerning how you spend your relational capital. Because as momma said, "Spend it wisely,' cause when it's gone, it's gone!"

PART III

THE LOST ART OF LISTENING

"Most people do not listen
with the intent to understand;
they listen with the intent to reply."
—Stephen R. Covey

Can anyone tell me why listening is so difficult? I suppose there are many reasons, stemming from our interest level to our attention span. Whatever the nature of the challenge, you and I must become good at listening if we are going to reach this current generation. It must become a discipline that is practiced intentionally.

In this section of the book we highlight the skill of listening and its importance in shaping God-given potential. You will learn new skills that will help you stay focused on the person being coached. Above all, you will learn why listening is foundational to next generation coaching.

16

ONE SIZE DOESN'T FIT ALL

Respecting the Diversity of Humanity

"The simple act of paying positive attention to people has a great deal to do with productivity."
—Tom Peters

Recently, I received an interesting text message from my daughter in Missouri. The text stated that she had several pairs of new contact lenses that she no longer needed. The reason for the extra pairs was that she had had Lasik surgery on her eyes and no longer needed them. They were taking up space on the shelves.

Being an occasional wearer of contact lenses, my first response was, "Wow! This is great." I actually got excited thinking I would not need to buy any for my summertime activities. Then it dawned on me that contact lenses are not a one-size-fits-all product. As it turned out, none of them fit my eyes.

Coaching is much like that experience. It is not one-size-fits-all. Why? Because we deal with human beings, and there are no two alike.

As a person in the business of shaping human lives, you have to learn to value the diversity of every human being, especially when it comes to passing on our personal convictions and philosophies.

As already stated in a previous chapter, it is important to honor individual differences. It is the uniqueness of every human that actually glorifies and magnifies the greatness of God. Sure we can learn from each other, but there are some things you will do different than I. Some of my methodology will seem awkward to you, and vice versa. My cognitive processes may differ from yours. Essentially, it's the same principle as Saul trying to make David use his armor (1 Samuel 17:39). It doesn't fit.

Remember the following advice when trying to pass along your experience to someone else.

1. Don't try to fix people the first time you meet them.

One of the greatest needs of the human soul is simply to be heard. Have you ever heard someone say, "No one understands me." That is often simply a cry to be heard. Instead of trying to "fix" the person, learn to listen and affirm them. Let the individual express himself, whether right or wrong. Only then can you minister to him. Remember, ministry must flow; it can't be forced.

2. Don't try to rubber stamp yourself on anyone.

As alluded to in an earlier chapter, it is easy for coaches and mentors to rubberstamp themselves on others; however, it becomes an exercise in futility, because there is only one you. When God created you, He threw the mold away and said, "I'll never do that again!" Yes, pass on the good things from your life, but better yet, lead people on a journey of discovering who God created them to be.

3. Don't assume people are incompetent just because they don't do what you do.

Diversity is seen in creation. It magnifies God's creative ability and shows his greatness.

Lest I be misunderstood and labeled a heretic, this is probably a good time for an explanation of diversity. By diversity I am not using it in the sense of an anything-goes policy. The Word of God is clear about ethical and moral issues, and we have no room to stretch the truth to accommodate diversity in sin.

Considering the culture-prone nature of mankind, it's easy to assume that just because someone doesn't play by the same culturally-accepted rules we do, they are somehow invaluable. Nonsense!

Honoring the uniqueness of individuals is what makes me so passionate about the coaching paradigm. It seeks to draw out that God-given potential instead of rubber-stamping individuals so they can be like me.

Have you learned to respect the uniqueness of others? It's the only way to coach members of the emerging generation to find and embrace their God-given potential.

17

CAN YOU HEAR ME NOW?

Grasping the Power of Listening Well

"I think that people just have this core desire to express who they are. And I think that's always existed."

—Mark Zuckerberg

You have probably seen the Verizon commercial where the service technician is testing the new Verizon Network in various locations and keeps repeating the phrase, "Can you hear me now?" As a spinoff, that question has become somewhat of a cultural buzzword. Although most of us know what it means, it symbolizes the idea of communication; that is, talking and listening.

Listening is a relatively simple skill everyone routinely practices, right? Actually, no! In today's culture many people have a hard time holding a normal conversation without periodically texting or checking their Facebook accounts. Ouch!

According to sociologists, much of the younger generation has an extreme deficit when it comes to listening and commonly used social skills. Research now suggests that frequent users of the social media tend to be lonely, have deviant values, and lack to some extent the emotional and social skills characteristic of high EI.[16]

Most experts agree that listening happens primarily on three levels: self-centered listening, other-centered listening, and intuitive listening. Each level has a function and includes rules and expectation all its own. Let's explore them.

1. Self-Centered Listening

Nothing is inherently wrong with this grade of listening; however, it is the lowest form of listening because it is motivated by self-interests. In other words, I am listening because I find the topic interesting or personally engaging. For instance, I watch ESPN because I desire to find out what is happening in the sports world. That is perfectly legitimate on one level; but if I were to listen to my coaching clients at this level, I might miss important bits of conversation, especially if it does not relate to me personally. When we listen only at this level, we tend to disconnect when the topic does not appeal to us.

2. Other-Centered Listening

This type of listening is a step up from self-centered listening. Here, we are not listening simply because it interests us but rather out of concern or care for others. Listening at this level is often a discipline, or, should we say, a labor of love.

Not all conversations are interesting. Plus, no one is *always* emotionally or physically able to listen intently 24/7; therefore, listening becomes an issue of intentionality.

3. Intuitive Listening

At this level, the coach not only hears what is being said, he also reads between the lines. This means he is looking for red flags things that do not sit just right or inconsistencies. Once areas of concern are spotted, a skilled coach will pursue and explore them, with the client's permission, of course.

The bottom line is that not every person will tell you exactly what he or she would like to say. Sometimes the subject is too painful. Maybe pride is involved, and transparency does not come easily; therefore, an effective coach must listen carefully and learn to read between the lines.

The next generation is crying out, and here is the essence of their plea: "Can you hear me now?" Learn to listen well. It can be extremely encouraging to them as they move toward their God-given destiny.

18

IS ANYBODY OUT THERE LISTENING?

Listening To Change the World

"Friends are those rare people
who ask how we are and then
wait to hear the answer."

—Ed Cunningham

Author and lecturer Margret J. Wheatley was onto something big when she said: "I believe we can change the world if we start listening to one another again. Simple, honest, human conversation."[17]

Could it really be that simple? Probably not, but it is true that powerful conversations do have potential to change lives. In order for conversations to become powerful, there must be a listening component.

Various questions emerge when we talk about listening. The usual argument about the subject goes like this: "Is the ability to listen a learned skill or an innate ability?" That's a good question. Undoubtedly, certain personality types have a deeper propensity for listening; however, I lean toward the premise that listening is a skill that can be learned, developed, and improved. Here's how it's done:

1. Be fully present when engaging in conversation.

True listening is the art of fully engaging someone; that is, being entirely present during the conversation. This practice is rare in today's world.

To be fully present in a conversation is a powerful force that has life-changing consequences for the person being engaged. Listening with this kind of intensity demands not only a measure of self-denial but also some learning and much practice.

Being fully engaged in conversation always makes the person feel more affirmed, valued, and supported. When full engagement is not offered, the opposite is true.

Are you fully present in your conversations?

2. Learn to listen to others merely to support them.

As a trained life coach, I have learned that the number one distraction from true listening is typically the strong urge to offer solutions. According to life coach Patrick Williams, this often distorts communication by superimposing the coach's agenda into the conversation and sidetracking it from the real issues.[18]

It's odd how we have a tendency to want to fix everyone. I'm not implying we can't and shouldn't help people, but what usually happens is that we train people to depend on us to do their thinking, thus creating followers not leaders.

How long has it been since you have listened in a supportive role? Can you imagine the impact this would have on a teenager, your spouse, or anyone else who might need a listening ear?

Learn to listen merely to support.

3. Learn to listen holistically.

This means listening with your entire being. Let the person know they have your undivided attention by sending signals with your body language, such as a frequent nod, leaning into the conversation, and maintaining eye contact.

Conversation is a two-way street; you either squelch it or encourage it by your body language. People aren't ignorant; they can read between the lines.

Do you give clues to others that you are listening? Be an active listener listen holistically.

4. Learn to listen intuitively.

Look for red flags in the conversation, signals that raise concerns. It could be something as simple as a hesitation in the conversation or as pronounced as tears or heightened emotions. Whatever invokes something inside the person could possibly be an intuition indicator.

Intuition indicators typically need to be explored. They are clues, often leading the way to an area that needs processing or probing more deeply. I've learned that if you listen long enough, people generally will reveal areas of pain or need, either covertly or overtly.

We must learn to spot the clues. If we don't we'll always catch ourselves saying, "I didn't see that coming."

Have you learned to really listen to people in a holistic way? Unfortunately, most of us lack in the development of this important skill.

19

READING BETWEEN THE LINES

The Art of Intuitive Listening

"There's something in
everyone only they know."

—Ben Harper

Have you ever seen the artist's drawing depicting what a paradigm shift might resemble? It's one picture that can be viewed as two, depending on what and where you focus. Usually, the line drawing is of an old hag or a beautiful woman. Sometimes it's a picture of either a duck or a rabbit. Same picture; two different ways of seeing it.

That describes how we need to treat coaching conversations. Often in a coaching session, one thought is vocalized; however, the person probably hopes you can read between the lines and recognize what he really wants to say.

Experts tell us that up to 90 percent of all conversation is driven by body language, voice tone and inflection, and expressions. This means potentially only 10 percent of communication in the real world is word driven. Since this is true, the coach must become a master at "reading between the lines."

Here are a few communication clues I have discovered over the years:

- Body language
- Strong emotion
- Repeated items
- Something that just doesn't sound right
- Pauses, sighs, and other emotional expressions

Although it sounds easy, spotting intuition indicators can be much like walking a tight rope stretched between the notion of suspicion and extreme trust. Sometimes, what you might think you are seeing or hearing isn't actually true. It's also possible to "be on-to-something" and not have the courage to ask about it.

So reading between the lines is a big part of what we do as coaches. Have you cultivated this skill? It is part of what we do as we develop God-given potential in members of the succeeding generation.

20

HAVE YOU CROSSED THE ROAD YET?

Getting Your Client To Venture Into New Territory

> "I was afraid of the Internet... because I couldn't type."
>
> —Jack Welch

This question is going to date me, but do you recall the song released in the early 70s titled, "Dead Skunk in the Middle of the Road"? It is a humorous ditty made popular by Wainwright Loudon from Great Britain. I remember that as a teenager the song somewhat amused me; however, the real message of the song is this: crossing the road can be dangerous!

Often, in the search for potential, we have to lead the person we are coaching "across the road," so to speak, in the discovery process. That road-crossing could be a step back in time, or, in some cases, it could be gazing into their future. Either way, it can be dangerous because it moves the client out of his comfort zone and into the unknown.

How do we help the client cross the road? I have found the following rules effective in this process.

1. Approach with caution.

Numerous obstacles on the road can prove fatal. Memories, fears, and unwanted emotions are powerful forces that can crush your client if you aren't careful. Approach with caution and let the person being coached take small steps as needed.

2. Look both ways.

Sometimes the person we are coaching must be prepped before this process can occur successfully. Warnings such as "pain ahead," "some discomfort may occur," or "fasten your seatbelt" need to be observed and noted. In so doing, we forewarn the person and lessen the blow.

3. Assure the client you will make the trip together.

It is much easier to navigate rough times when you have company along. Oh yeah, did I mention that it is generally a good idea to ask permission before crossing the road? Getting the client's okay to address sensitive issues is a must. When we do, the experience is perceived as help from God rather than a trespass.

Have you helped your client cross the road? Be prepared. It can be dangerous.

21

I DON'T THINK THEY GET IT!

Addressing Awareness and
Responsibility Issues

"Be candid with everyone."

—Jack Welch

As a life coach, you will often find yourself stuck in your dealings with spiritual sons and daughters. When this happens, you must ask yourself the question, "Should I press the issue or just let it go?"

I can't tell you how many times I have been at this crossroad. As a good coach, you too will find yourself at this point sooner or later during the coaching relationship. Inevitably issues will surface and need to be resolved, so the coach must become skilled at addressing these concerns with accuracy and proper timing. How does one do this? Where is the starting point for determining if the snag is a constraint holding the person back from reaching his potential?

For starters, every coach must become skilled at what Susan Scott calls Interrogating Reality.[19] By simple definition, she is referring to the art of getting to the bottom of issues. What is the root problem? Who is at fault? Why is this happening? That is the starting point.

For the client, it is often a matter of not being able to see the forest for the trees. Through the simple coaching skill of revisiting emotional issues, the coach can help the person process what's really happening and get to the bottom of it.

In the process of revisiting an issue, you will sometimes discover that the client is oblivious to the issue. He simply doesn't recognize it as a problem. Everybody else around him may spot it, but he doesn't.

In light of the fact that every person has blind spots, awareness can never be taken for granted. Awareness can be discerned in several ways, but primarily the easiest way is through the use of a 360-degree assessment test. This test allows the client to grade himself in certain areas. Those who work closest with him also grade him on the same areas. The results often reveal a huge gap between how the client sees himself and how his associates, friends, and family view him. The results can be eye-opening.

Once awareness is discovered, responsibility is the next hurtle. It is not uncommon in coaching situations to discover that the client is unwilling to take personal responsibility for an issue. This presents another set of problems that basically come down to one or two ways of engagement. We won't spend much time on the subject other than to say it is either a growth issue or a rebellion issue. A growth issue can relate to maturity or character. A matter of rebellion is more of a sin problem. Each is dealt with differently.

If you've ever said, "I don't think they get it," you could be right! This is a common issue in coaching.

22

GETTING INSIDE THE MIND OF YOUR CLIENT

The Power of Intuition Indicators

"The intuitive mind is a sacred gift and the rational mind is a faithful servant. We have created a society that honors the servant and has forgotten the gift."

—Albert Einstein

A well-marked road always has signs indicating what lies ahead. Arrows, shapes, and diagrams are only a few of the signals that show us the way. A user-friendly road helps us navigate the twists, turns, and detours without problems.

We can apply this same idea to coaching. I have discovered that most clients are predisposed at displaying signals that something just isn't right in the conversation. These signs often lie just below the surface of the discussion or topic at hand. The trained coach can pick up on them in a heartbeat and carefully explore them for important clues. In the coaching arena these are called intuition indicators.[20]

An intuition indicator could be a word, action or inflection that sets off an alarm in your mind. Call it a red flag, something amiss, whatever; it's that subtle hint that something is wrong.

In coaching, we use these clues to get inside our clients' heads.

The following are examples of intuition indicators:

- You are coaching someone when right in the middle of the conversation, a tear wells up, or the client becomes emotional and his voice breaks.
- The client repeats an item or says the same thing over and over.
- He or she manifests body language that conveys a disposition or attitude.

These are all clues that once they are noticed, need to be probed because underneath the surface often lies a need to be met. As coaches we always get the client's permission to address what we perceive to be intuition indicators. When this happens the client perceives your probing to be assistance instead of a trespass.

Finally, it is important to understand that when we talk about intuition indicators we are not necessarily referring to spiritual discernment. Although God can show you something supernaturally, these intuition indicators can simply be natural responses that can be easily missed.

Are you trained and skilled at picking up on intuition indicators?

23

COACHING WITH EMPTY HANDS

Learning To Lay Aside Your Agenda

"Never question another man's motive. His wisdom, yes, but not his motives."

—Dwight Eisenhower

As discussed in a previous chapter, listening is a skill we, typically, have not appreciated and cultivated. Short of good feedback, we are usually left to determine our own listening ability; therefore, many of us hold an exaggerated opinion of our listening skills. My wife claims I have what she calls, "selective hearing." Personally, I think it's a disorder found primarily in men.

Seriously, most of us could use a little more development in the area of listening skills. Yes, I said *skills*. You see, I believe listening is an ability anyone can learn and nurture. Of course, people with certain personality temperaments are naturally better at it, but any person can improve in this area.

We must learn to approach every conversation as if it were important, simply because it might be. In her book, *Fierce Conversations,* Susan Scott teaches us that life succeeds or fails one conversation at a time.

Here are several ideas to help you with your listening skills.

1. Lay aside your "I-know-the-answer" attitude.

When you think you have the solution, it is easy to disconnect cognitively, plus it becomes impossible to listen deeply and thoroughly (intuitively).

2. Listen with your heart not merely with your head.

Many thoughts flow from the heart, including compassion, concern, and empathy, to mention a few. Most of your coaching clients need this type of affirmation to grow and face the painful places in life.

3. Don't let the "I'm-an-expert-in-my-field" mentality take over.

Believe me, when the person you are coaching appears on the radar screen of your own experience, it's easy to switch to auto-pilot as your expert mentality kicks in. When this happens, we are prone to quench the creativity of the Holy Spirit. God may be trying to reveal something to the person you are coaching, in which case, you simply become the facilitator of what God is doing. Don't mess it up by running on "expert" auto-pilot.

Coaching with empty hands simply means you are not trying to run ahead in the conversation. How can you listen if you are down the road or off track in your thoughts? Coaching with empty hands means you remove your "telling hat" and simply listen in a non-judgmental way. There will be a time to "tell" but not when you are trying to listen.

So listening must become a discipline an intentional practice. No one ever becomes a good listener accidently.

The lack of good listeners in our culture is one of the greatest issues of our time. Every soul has an innate need to be heard. That need can be met only through meaningful relationships forged through meaningful conversations.

Not every individual wants to be fixed immediately; rather, he or she just wants to be heard.

PART IV

ASKING POWERFUL QUESTIONS

"The important thing is
not to stop questioning.
Curiosity has its own reason
for existing."

—Albert Einstein

Asking too many questions is unacceptable in our society. People prefer answers rather than questions; however, powerful questions are the key to evoking deep thought and resolution in others. Questions are also vital to developing self-awareness in others, and they can draw people into a conversation like nothing else.

In this section you will be introduced to the use of powerful questions and the role they play in coaching the next generation. You'll learn how to craft open-ended questions and how to follow your curiosity through the use of questions. These tools are foundational for the effective coach.

24

QUESTIONING
THE PROCESS

The Use of Questions In Life Coaching

"Socrates told us, 'The
unexamined life is not worth living.'
I think he's calling for curiosity,
more than knowledge. In every
human society at all times and
at all levels, the curious are
at the leading edge."
—Roger Ebert

Powerful questions receive little veneration in the Western world. Most of us are looking for answers. I understand why this is so, but could it also be that probing questions become the substance that connects the cognitive thought process to the problem? I believe so.

The Creator designed the human mind in such a way as to engage or kick in when it encounters the unknown, much like clicking the "search button" on your internet browser or hitting "okay" on a dialogue box. Well-framed questions engage the brain and start the search process.

It is possible that an answer may be couched within this type of question. Jesus surely thought so. He used questions in conversation every day. His wise use of queries expanded the conversation rather than narrowing it and became a powerful tool used to provoke thought in dialogue. We too must learn this technique if we are to succeed at coaching spiritual sons and daughters.

The skillful coach uses questions not merely to gain information but to evoke deeper thought in people. The gospels record Jesus asking over 300 questions. It wasn't because He was ignorant. He inquired to motivate deeper learning and self- awareness in the life of those He encountered.

"Who do you say that I am?" "Do you understand what I have done to you?" "What is it that you want me to do for you?" Do you recognize any of these examples? Each is a conversation-evoking question for which Jesus already knew the answer. He used them intentionally to cause His encounters with others to become thought provoking and unforgettable. He understood that life has the potential to succeed or fail one conversation at a time. Do you?

Coaches must learn to question the processes of life, to use powerful questions to evoke deeper learning. Learn to follow your curiosity as a coach. When things don't seem to add up, probe. Ask questions, draw out explanations, and make people think deeply about their situations in life. Progress, freedom, and growth will result.

25

THE "COLUMBO" FACTOR

Four Types of Questions to Use When Coaching Sons and Daughters

"The starting point is a question."

—Albert Manguel

The late Peter Falk starred in "Columbo," a long-running detective series in the '80s. Falk, as Columbo, gained notoriety for his twist on solving crimes. Robed in a rumpled old overcoat and with a cigar stub clinched between his lips, he often asked what appeared at first to be "stupid" questions. His intent, however, was to focus on an angle that was missing in the investigation or to point out an aspect of the crime that had been overlooked. And his tactics worked, most of the time.

In much the same way, asking powerful questions is the hallmark for coaching.[21] It's key to exploration and discovery. A well-crafted and appropriate query posed at the right time has the uncanny ability to focus attention on vague issues and prompt the person you are coaching to make choices and take actions. Every coach must master this skill if he hopes to draw out God-given potential from his clients.

In order to be most effective, coaches must learn to ask what we call open-ended questions—those queries that require more than a simple yes or no answer. For the skilled coach, closed questions are taboo for they tend to narrow the conversation, while open-ended questions broaden it.

A skilled coach must learn to ask four types of questions (each one open-ended), depending on the conversation and the need of the moment. Here is a brief overview of each.

1. Direct Questions[22]

Direct questions get immediately to the core of the matter. They are aimed at the heart to pierce defenses and jar the person to conclusions. They can be breathtaking, perhaps even catching the client off guard.

Asking direct questions naturally depends on your level of relational capital. The coach must determine if the person being coached is ready for such a question; otherwise, the relationship might be breached. Direct questions fit into the category described by the Proverb: "…Faithful are the wounds of a friend." They are often considered to be the secret weapon of coaching.

2. Open Questions

An open question is one that unbolts the door for the person you are coaching to visit an area of thinking heretofore unconsidered. Do not confuse open questions with open-ended questions. Each of the four types listed here is open-ended.

An open question might begin as follows: "What would it look like if …?" You just swung open the door for the client to go somewhere new in his thinking. Observe his response and follow your curiosity from there.

3. Ownership Questions

Ownership questions force the person being coached to assume responsibility; to take action in his situation, whether or not it is his fault. In coaching sessions, people often try to blame other people, situations, and scenarios for their own unwise choices. You will hear, "I wasn't reared properly; I have little education; or, my boss is the problem." Some of these excuses may be based on fact, but the person being coached can't change the third party.

Ownership questions are powerful with regard to evoking personal responsibility for future actions.

4. Revealing Questions

This type of inquiry helps the client shed new light on a situation or think in a different vein. A revealing question might look something like this: "What would you be doing right now, if you had plenty of money, time, education, etc.?

Revealing questions help get the person "unstuck" by prompting him to look beyond his present status. They release "creative juices" in the human brain, causing it to perform as it was created to perform—to think!

Questions serve numerous purposes in coaching. They can open up and expand an area, or they can help probe and intensify a person's focus. Jesus used questions in nearly all of His conversations. In essence, each of His conversations was a coaching session.

Have you learned to use powerful questions? Have you mastered the fab-four mentioned above?

26

OPENING THE DOOR BUT NOT LEADING THE WAY

Asking the Right Questions

"If we ask the right questions
we can change the world."

—Dessler Systems

Asking "leading questions" is a cardinal sin for those of us in the coaching industry. This occurs when a coach wraps or disguises a suggestion in a question. For example, "Have you thought about going to your boss with that?" or "Why don't you just talk to them about it?"

To the untrained ear, these kinds of questions seem innocuous. And, of course, occasions arise when it is appropriate and even necessary to speak into a person's life. So what is wrong with asking leading questions in the search for potential? The main problem is that leading questions tend to squelch the discovery process and have a tendency to produce followers rather than leaders. This type of inquiry doesn't prompt the individual to stretch; instead, it allows him to remain in his spiritual, emotional, and cognitive comfort zone.

A skilled coach will crack open the door to an unexplored area of the client's life without the use of leading questions. Here's what that would look like: as I'm coaching a person, I recognize important information can be gleaned by visiting a particular area of his life. So, I ease the door ajar with an open question (see the list of question types provided in the previous chapter) then observe how the client reacts to my invitation to go there. We call this the OPS model.[23]

The OPS model is a great tool to use in helping clients explore. Simply open the door with a question, then observe, probe, and sift:

1. **Observe**—Watch the client's response.

2. **Probe**—Follow your curiosity, according to the client's response, and go deeper, if needed.

3. **Sift**—Assess whether you and the person are on the right track. Ask yourself, "Is this a rabbit trail? Do we need to go here?"

The key to using the OPS model is asking open questions with skill. Here is another example of an open question. "What might it look like if you went to your boss about this?" versus a leading question: "Have you thought about going to your boss?"

See how it works? An open question simply cracks the door for exploration in a certain area. It lets the client choose whether or not to go there. Be sure not to confuse an open question with an open-ended question. All good coaching questions are open-ended, but not all are open questions.

Have you learned how to open doors for others; not natural doors but doors that lead to areas that need to be addressed or explored? Try it; it could be life changing for the person you are coaching.

27

HELPING THE CLIENT WITH THE FORENSIC WORK

Learning to Read Between the Lines

"How many things have to happen to you before something occurs to you?"

—Robert Frost

I am a huge fan of "NCIS,"[24] a television show I began watching several years ago while staying with a friend in Tulsa during my doctoral training. He recorded an episode on his DVR, and we sat down one evening to watch it. I was hooked! Now I rarely miss a telecast. I think my fondness for the show stems from the characters' use of "forensics" in solving crimes.

The term *forensic* refers to the method of finding evidence or proof regarding an incident or happening by using fingerprint analysis, DNA, or some other discovery of a scientific nature. As a coach, you too will find forensic-type clues lying dormant in your clients. These hints often point to their God-given potential.

God always leaves clues wherever He has been. Those hints are sometimes hidden in life experiences or buried beneath mounds of circumstances. To the person being coached, they may appear to be whimsical or meaningless. As a coach, you are to lead the client on a search and rescue mission to recover hidden clues.

In the natural, several elements must come together in order for a forensics team to uncover valuable clues. First, a thorough search must be conducted within the borders of the designated area. This is why in coaching we always return to the client's life experiences. That is where the boundaries of the search can be found.

Second, it is important to note that clues rarely show up without a strategic search being initiated. Every inch of the marked off scene is examined, several times, if necessary. Any evidence is recorded and documented immediately. You, too, as a coach, need to search for evidence. Going back over the client's life experience can reveal a mountain of signals that God has been there.

Finally, it is imperative that certain tools—a magnifying glass or microscope and electronic devices—are available to aid in the search. The technology used in forensics is always state-of-the-art. Likewise, the coach has various tools (God's Word, teaching resources, books, and videos, to name a few) at his disposal to help him in coaching spiritual sons and daughters. And, don't forget the coach's toolkit, which includes the skills learned through coaching certification and training.

Once discovered, clues need to be analyzed and recorded so accurate conclusions can be drawn in light of other properties at the scene. Individual clues may not make sense until they are viewed in light of other evidence.

God has left many clues hidden in the ruins of your past. These traces need to be discovered because they add texture and design to the fabric God is weaving through your life.

How about helping your sons and daughters revisit a highly emotional experience? It could unearth clues to help them on their spiritual journey.

Bottom line: don't try to solve every riddle for those you are coaching. Help them see God at work in all things.

28

WHAT DID YOU MEAN BY THAT?

The Use of Good Feedback in Coaching

"It's as simple as this. When people don't unload their opinions and feel like they've been listened to, they won't really get on board."

—Patrick Lencioni

My good friend, Dr. Joseph Umidi, founder and president of Lifeforming Leadership Coaching, calls feedback "the breakfast of champions."

Feedback is a lost gift in many circles, basically because we have not welcomed it with enthusiasm. We have assumed that by virtue of our expertise or calling we are immune from error. Nothing could be farther from the truth.

Effective leaders know that accurate feedback is necessary if they are to lead with clarity and precision. Feedback is a method by which we collect information from others then relate it back to them in order to bring greater awareness to them.

As a coach, you must never assume you are tracking with the person you are coaching. I've heard it said that assumptions are always made for the advantage of those doing the assuming.

Here are a few tips on giving and receiving feedback:

1. Ask the person to repeat back to you what they hear you saying.

Since information passes through a person's human grid of thinking, meaning and clarity are easily lost in conversation. It is acceptable to ask the person being coached to repeat back to you what you just explained.

2. Explain to the person you are coaching that *anytime* is the right time to offer feedback.

This rule is usually established up front in a coaching relationship. If the client waits too long to offer or ask for feedback, the information becomes stale and impotent. A word spoken in due season is like a beautiful picture in settings of gold and silver (see Proverbs 25:11).

3. Allow the client to offer written feedback.

Written comments are invaluable; many of the individuals you coach will be able to write their feedback clearer than they could verbalize it. That is why I always allow the person I am coaching to send me unlimited emails.

Permit me to offer a note of caution here: It is often easy for the person you are coaching to say more than is needed when giving feedback in written form alone. Coach your clients to use the utmost care in giving written responses.

Feedback is necessary for the leader's progress. It allows two people to be on the same wave length and usually keeps misunderstandings to a minimum.

Where are you with regard to feedback? You should be both giving and receiving it.

29

THE FLIPSIDE OF FEEDBACK

Learning To Receive Feedback

"A wonderful gift may not be wrapped as you expect."

—Jonathan Lockwood Huie

Not only is feedback good for the client, it is also accommodating for the coach. We often assume too much concerning our progress with those we are coaching, and, occasionally, we can be way off base. Most people engaged in the process recoil from divulging how they really feel about their coaching experience. That reticence may be resolved by encouraging them to respond with feedback.

How does one go about receiving constructive feedback?

1. Ask for it.

"How do you think we're doing?" "Are you seeing the results you were expecting from the coaching experience?" These types of questions allow your clients to share without being considered rude. Inviting feedback puts them at ease about sharing their responses.

If you don't welcome feedback, people will refrain from offering it.

2. Good feedback generally comes from those closest to you.

When soliciting personal feedback related to your work, consider asking those who know you best: your wife, boss, or best friend. The most valuable feedback generally comes from your inner circle—those who know you best and love you most. They are conscious of your blind spots, but they generally won't discharge that information until asked.

3. Accept all feedback, negative and positive, with grace.

Of course, not all the feedback you receive will be accurate. Most people miss the bulls-eye, but they rarely miss the entire target. If it's important enough for them to tell you, pay attention.

4. If the feedback is vague, ask for specifics.

Specificity becomes the litmus test for all useful feedback. If it can be specified, pay attention. If not, it may simply be criticism or mud-slinging.

If you want to connect with a client and keep the coaching experience moving forward, make room for feedback. The process has to be a two-way street.

30

QUESTIONING FROM A NON-JUDGMENTAL STANCE

Asking the Right Questions To Probe the Situation

"There are some questions that shouldn't be asked until a person is mature enough to appreciate the answers."

—Anne Bishop

I cannot overstate the importance of powerful questions in the process of helping our spiritual sons and daughters reach their God-given potential. This ancient/modern principle is often viewed as counter-intuitive in this information age; however, when it is understood and applied properly, amazing results can transpire.

One of the most important points to remember about questions is that they must be offered in a non-judgmental way if they are to be effective. Being non-judgmental serves a dual purpose: (1) it allows the person you are coaching to feel safe enough to share, and (2) it helps the coach to be flexible and open in following his curiosity and probing for truth.

Here are a few tips that will help you ask non-weighted questions:

1. Ask "what" and "how" more than "why."

What and how questions open the door of exploration for most people. "Why" questions tend to raise defenses in the person being coached, especially in volatile situations. Instead of asking, "Why did you do that?" Ask, "What do you think lead you to respond that way?"

It may sound like a minor issue, but these kinds of questions disarm most people, allowing them to relax and feel concern rather than being distracted and stressed.

2. Watch your choice of words and voice tone when asking powerful questions.

Pitch and fervor are pivotal in how conversation is perceived. The volume of your voice also makes a difference. Pay close attention to the emotion, or lack thereof, you convey with your words. Feeling can be communicated as clearly as your verbal message.

Practicing these skills can keep your coaching conversations from being hijacked; from becoming a fulfillment of your agenda rather than your client's. Staying focused allows the person being coached to think for himself and become empowered to deal with the issues; to take responsibility.

Of course you can speak into the client's life, but only after you have helped him exercise his own cognitive muscles. By doing this, you will be producing wisdom in his life rather than folly. Isn't that what you want?

31

GETTING ONE'S HEAD ON STRAIGHT

The Power of Reframing Success

> "Failure is the condiment
> that gives success its flavor."
>
> —Truman Capote

Having an accurate understanding of success is essential for today's emerging leaders. In our world success is often measured in terms of material possessions and popularity; this, however, is a faulty gauge.

In the coaching arena, it's not uncommon to find individuals whose concept of success is a bit skewed and in need of "tweaking." One of the goals of coaching a person to reach his God-given potential is helping him "get his head on straight" with regard to success and failure.

In coaching, we call this process the "reframing of success." It isn't as easy as it sounds, for more often than not the coach must deal with years of erroneous thinking. Deep set values of this nature don't change overnight.

We generally begin by guiding the person in examining or defining his core values. It is essential that he understands exactly what he prizes and how it impacts his life. In the natural, the infrastructure of a building determines its overall soundness. The same is true with our lives.

Whether one realizes it or not, every person orders his life according to his core values. Many of our habits, likes and dislikes are shaped by our value systems.

A definitive way to detect an individual's core values is to observe his life patterns. For instance, my wife values frugality. She wastes nothing. She isn't a hoarder; she just hates to waste anything, ranging from her time to the last bite of food on the table. I have seen her store a tidbit of food in a Zip-lock bag and save it for later, when I would have tossed it. This pattern of frugality is obvious in every area of her life.

Your life patterns reveal your core values, especially in the area of success and failure.

Some values are what I call "hand-me-downs." These are those life issues that have been imposed on you by others. Perhaps your parents forced them on you; or you may have learned them as a means of attracting attention or getting your way. Whatever the case, you acquired them under some kind of pressure, and now they are ingrained in your life.

A gifted coach will guide his or her spiritual sons and daughters in discovering these patterns and what triggers them and will help them plan a proactive course of action. Healthy conclusions can be realized.

Getting one's head on straight is important. Dealing with symptoms and behavior will never get the job done; it's the issues of the heart that matter.

32

FOLLOWING YOUR CURIOSITY

The Fun Side of Coaching

> "The mind is not a vessel to be filled, but a fire to be kindled."
> —Plutarch

You've heard the old saying, "Curiosity killed the cat." That adage probably originated as a warning. I've discovered that a healthy dose of curiosity may indeed get you into trouble; however, the skilled coach must allow himself to follow his curiosity if he hopes to move people toward their God-given potential.

For many trainees, this is one of the most challenging aspects of coaching, primarily because they have not learned to trust the process. Our culture has programed us to rush to judgment and quickly "fix" the situation. The "fix-it" paradigm has its place, especially if one is mentoring or counseling, but it does not work well in the coaching model.

So, for starters, the coach in training has to lay aside his fix-it mentality and listen for topics that need further investigation or discussion. Most people know subconsciously and will tell the coach where they need to begin, if he will simply pay attention and follow his natural curiosity.

Second, the coach must learn to hear more than is being said (see the previous chapter). In coaching circles, this is known as observing—being fully tuned in, not trying to force your own agenda. Allow yourself to be curious about why the client said something or acted in a particular way. Question any response that seems out of the ordinary. Pick up on nuances that may be clues leading to the resolution of the issue.

The model we use when following our curiosity is known as the OPS,[25] an acronym for Observe, Probe, and Sift. When we observe, we are alert to subliminal messages in body language, tone of voice, hesitancies, or a show of emotion or lack thereof. To help the client discover his God-given potential, the coach must learn to observe.

The next part of the model is to probe, which opens the door for the client to examine or discuss something you may have noticed or sensed. Probing is done by asking what we call an "open question." This in turn opens the door for the client to enter that area. Then you simply observe again the response to see if your hunch was correct.

The final part of the OPS model is to sift; decide if what you are seeing (curiosity) and probing is accurate. You may be "chasing rabbits," or you could be projecting your own experience into that area.

Do you recognize the importance of following your curiosity? Have you learned to do that? It's a great way to help your client discover his God-given potential. Try it you might like it.

PART V

KNOW THYSELF

"The greatest thing in the world
is to know how to belong to oneself."

—Michel de Montaigne

Self-awareness is a moot topic in Evangelical circles today, primarily because the word *self* is associated with egotism and self-centeredness, which, of course, is an important biblical subject. Being self-absorbed is a problem; however the term *self-awareness* is not the same as *self-centeredness*.

Self-awareness is the idea that humanity has a God-given ability to look inside and think about what is happening in the emotions, thoughts, and feelings. In coaching, we call it *meta-cognition*, which literally means, "to think about what you are thinking about."

In this section we will address the importance of self-awareness and its role in both discovering and developing one's God-given potential.

33

HOW DID I KNOW THAT?

The Importance of Self-Awareness in the Coaching Environment

"I know of no other man I'd rather be than who I am."

—Bishop T.D. Jakes

Do you have a clear picture of your current reality? I certainly hope you do because clarity is power. Self-awareness is inextricably linked with clarity.

God created mankind in His own image. Our Creator designed us as triune beings consisting of spirit, soul, and body. One might ask, "If this trinity of mankind is inseparable, how can it be explained?" The theological and behavioral aspect of the trinity of mankind will be examined deeper in a succeeding chapter, however suffice it to say that the *soul* of mankind is the seat of self, the personality of man.

It is the soulish component of Mankind's make-up that allows him to relate to himself. He can think about what he is thinking about—*meta-cognition.* He has the ability to understand and process information about himself; things like strengths, weaknesses, emotions, feelings, and passions. Self-awareness resides in the soul.

So the question arises, "Why is self-awareness so important in unleashing God-given potential?" Mainly because to have self-awareness simply means that the person has processed the situation with the help of a coach and has arrived at the clearest picture of the current reality. This is huge! It is a major step forward primarily because to have a clear picture means the person now has more choices from which to respond, rather than merely reacting.

Here are a few things that happen when you help people to gain self-awareness.

- They receive a heightened sense of awareness
- Insightful glimpses into their negative thoughts, feelings and emotions
- They journey into *their* way of being, i.e. self image
- Insight into ingrained patterns of sensing, feeling, thinking and behaving
- Heightened awareness of their perception of the current situation
- Insight into necessary changes that must be taken in order to move forward
- A new look at life and its challenges

Self-awareness is essential in unleashing the person being coached into their God-given potential. In fact, this component is so important God often uses self-awareness to show us what is in our own hearts and minds. For instance, God led the children of Israel through the desert to show them what was in their hearts. Unfortunately, most of them never really got it. They saw God's deeds while Moses understood God's ways (see Psalm 103:7, KJV).

As a coach, you must become proficient at evoking self-awareness in those you are coaching. Contrary to popular opinion it is not accomplished by only giving instructions and merely trying to fix people. (Again, I'm not against advice giving and fixing people!) Rather, it is better accomplished by following your curiosity and observing things that don't sit just right with you. Sensitive areas that are just below the surface level of normal conversation. Once these are discovered and permission is granted from the client, you can then walk them through the issue. Enlightenment is the result, both from the human spirit and from the Holy Spirit.

Jesus was a master at this, and His *modus operandi* was to use powerful questions. Have you learned the art of evoking deeper learning and self-awareness in the people you are coaching?

34

INTERIOR LANDSCAPING

The Art of Shaping the Inner Man

> "Rocks in my path?
> I keep them all.
> With them I shall build my castle."
>
> —Nemo Nox

What do you know about "interior landscaping"? If you're like me, you know very little about the topic. As a matter of fact, I only recently heard the term. I inadvertently picked up a book on leadership, and there it was in black and white.

Interior landscaping is a relatively new idiom being used by the secular world to describe, "getting in touch with your inner life." I suppose that would make all of us who are interested in the inner-life "interior landscapers." Right?

Jesus used metaphors like *fruit* and *trees* to describe one's inner character. "By their fruit you shall know them" (Matthew 7:20). He spoke of good trees and bad trees in relationship to character (Matthew 7:18), so I'd venture to say the term "interior landscaping" certainly applies. Whatever allegory you use really doesn't matter; what does matter is the fact that every person has his own unique potential that needs to be cultivated in order for him to become all God wants him to be.

With this in mind, the coach's job is to plow the soil of the human heart to provoke discovery. It's one thing for you, as a coach, to see and recognize it. It's totally another for the client to grasp it. It is not enough for the coach to tell the client he or she has potential. The person you are coaching must be able to discover that latent ability for himself. Then, and only then, will he be motivated to go for it. In the coaching paradigm, this incentive is awakened by using a variety of tools, each designed to evoke self-awareness in the client.

The term *self-awareness* describes the notion of being in touch with what's going on inside of oneself. In his groundbreaking book, *Working with Emotional Intelligence,* Daniel Goleman calls this quality EQ the ability to judge one's thoughts, feelings, and emotions and make judgment calls regarding them. Self-aware leaders are attuned to their inner signals.[26] Based on this illumination, self-awareness is a great gift from God.

Of all of God's creatures, human beings are the only ones who are capable of self-awareness. The animal kingdom possesses only a limited sense of self. A bird will never sit down and reason out whether or not it is time to fly south. No, it relies purely on instinct. Only humans, and I suppose angels, have a profound sense of self-awareness.

As coaches, our job is to evoke a more acute sense of self (and God) awareness in the persons we are coaching. This is done primarily through conversation and by asking powerful questions.

35

SELF-CONSCIOUSNESS VERSUS SELF-AWARENESS

Understanding Spirit, Soul, and Body

"If a man is to live, he must
be all alive, body, soul,
mind, heart, and spirit."

—Thomas Merton

Self-consciousness can be defined as an unhealthy preoccupation with what others think of us. Obsessive self-consciousness leads to fear, which can lead to paralysis and immobilization, among other hindrances.

Although they are related, self-consciousness and self-awareness are not to be confused. The Christian community at times seems apprehensive about self-awareness. We tend to associate it with egotism or narcissism; however, the term is in no way comparable to that notion.

God created mankind as triune beings consisting of spirit, soul, and body. The spirit component enables a person to relate to the unseen world—God, angels, and even the demonic realm. With the physical side of his make-up, he is capable of connecting with the physical world. He sees the colors of the sunset, feels the cool breeze, smells the flowers, and tastes the cool water. With the soul, he relates to himself. He recognizes who he is, how he is tempered, and understands his strengths or weaknesses. He can sense his feelings, emotions, and make judgment calls on each, either in favor of or against them.

God intended the soul of man to help him on his journey. Of course, the soul is subject to the spirit man, and the soul needs periodic renewal, which, of course, is another lesson altogether. God uses self-awareness to show us what is in our hearts and minds. He led the children of Israel through the dessert to reveal to them what was in their hearts, but they never fully grasped His purposes. Psalm 103 says, "He made known his ways to Moses, his deeds to the people of Israel" (v. 7).

Self-awareness is vital if your client is to discover his God-given potential. As a coach you must become skilled at the art of evoking this kind of search. A trip to the library will never produce it. "Googling" it will not evoke this level of learning. Jesus provoked this type of deeper learning by asking powerful questions. He was a master at it. You can do the same.

When probing issues of the soul, blind spots are inevitable. Like scars, we all have them. I've always said, "It would be a terrible thing to be a jerk and not know it!" If this is true, then developing self-awareness is crucial in discovering our God-given potential.

In unleashing our clients to discover their God-given potential, we must help them get in touch with their inner life. I personally believe that both self-awareness as well as God awareness must be cultivated. The human spirit has the ability to perceive and be enlightened, hence self-awareness. Also, it has the capacity to receive from God so it can be God-aware.

It's the place where the Holy Spirit resides, and this is where real transformation takes place.

Self-awareness occurs when the human spirit and soul are illuminated. Once this happens, motivation is no longer a problem. A light turns on and the person sees for himself. His experience is no longer hand-me-down or secondhand advice. He assumes ownership, which is a motivating force. True change finds it source in inner motivation, not from acquiring information.

There are several ways to evoke awareness in the person you are coaching; however, I believe the best place to begin is by using the *indirect method*—a gentle nudge from you, the coach, to help him move toward an obvious answer. The means we use is an *open question,* which simply opens the door for the person to explore a thought or area he has been closed to or unaware of heretofore.

The process might look something like this: "Tell me what would happen if you_____ (fill in the blank) (i.e., went to your boss; spoke with the authorities).

As coaches, you and I must improve our skill of evoking self-awareness in the next generation. Where will you start?

36

THE ART OF EXTRACTING LESSONS FROM LIFE

Learning From Experience

"Life is a succession
of lessons which must be lived
to be understood."

—Helen Keller

The skill of mining lessons from one's life is almost nonexistent today. It's a dying art for several reasons: (1) Most of us are too busy to reflect and learn. (2) The job of reflection is inner work; therefore, it is often more difficult than it sounds.

Gleaning from life simply means taking time to consider and learn from both our positive and negative experiences. The persons we are coaching need to digest the following principles, which will help them reflect and distill life's lessons.

1. God's will usually moves slower than you think it should.

God rarely operates according to our timetable. If you don't believe that, just ask Abraham, Job, or anyone else who has walked with Him for any length of time. If this is true and it is then patience and flexibility are great virtues.

Do you have the biblical quality of patience required to inherit the promises of God (see Hebrews 6:10)?

Whoa partner! Slow down and allow God to work by His own schedule, not yours.

2. All great people have great people in their lives.

What have you learned in the last six months from other great people? You can never become all God has destined you to be without great people in your life; people who aren't impressed with who you are, but who will tell you the truth and not back down.

Do you presently have these kinds of people in your life?

3. Knowing God is a journey.

What do you know about God that you didn't know this time last year? He is so awesome, He can't be known all at once. Why? He is greater than any one experience, and much more substantial than an event. He can't be captured merely by one's mind or feelings. Of course, part of that "knowing" comes to us by way of information supplied in books, the Holy Bible, and from preachers and teachers. But knowing Him intimately is an experience, a ride, and a journey.

Are you ready for it?

So what lessons are your clients gleaning from life and ministry? Lessons that are overlooked generally have to be revisited later in life, and who wants another trip around the same mountain?

Lady wisdom is always speaking, especially to those who will listen (see Proverbs 8). So teach others that every occurrence can and should be a learning experience.

37

SEARCHING FOR GOD CLUES

Developing the Art of Reflection in Others

"Follow effective action with quiet reflection. From the quiet reflection will come even more effective action."

—Peter Drucker

Reflection is a great tool to use when one is trying to uncover the clues God has put in his or her life. The art of reflection is the idea of garnering "God clues" from everyday life. It's often accomplished by unpacking emotional experiences in order to comprehend on a deeper level the lessons that give meaning and shape to life.

Many valuable lessons lie in the ruins of past experiences. If we can cultivate a "What-did-I-learn-from-that?" mentality, we can better understand what God is saying to us and also prevent repeatable mistakes and errors. Repeatedly in the Holy Scriptures we find God admonishing us to "remember" (see

Deuteronomy 5:15; 8:2; 9:7; 1 Chronicles 16:12; Exodus 20:8; Ephesians 2:11, 12).

So how do we practice a "searching mentality"? How is biblical reflection done and where do I start? Here are a few tips you can pass on to those with whom you work.

1. Learn to excavate life's painful moments.

Reflection is not for the weak at heart; it is hard work. Often the toil of recalling and reliving pain can be an emotional experience. As a coach, always obtain verbal permission before entering a sensitive area. If not, your efforts may be perceived as an intrusion when dealing with a painful issue. Keep in mind that powerful questions can unearth or arouse old, buried feelings. Be sensitive to these and offer support as the client walks through the pain.

2. Broaden your scope of the search.

A good look at the context of an experience can often help process the event. What was the context in which the event took place? Was I tired? What was my stress level at the time? Was God in this or was it self-induced? These and other powerful pieces can help the client garner the clues he or she may need to make sense of life.

3. Ask for God's perspective on the situation.

God's perspective on a situation is often just "one thought away." Finding that one thought or gesture could provide the freedom one is seeking; however, revealing that one "God thought" can be challenging. Ask God for that one thought that changes everything.

Most of us seldom slow down long enough to analyze the emotional experiences of life, so we find ourselves going over and over the same ground.

Could this have been what Jacob was practicing when he awoke from sleep and revisited his dream? Upon reflection he came to a startling realization: "Surely the Lord is in this place, and I was not aware of it" (Genesis 28:16).

Can you imagine what we've missed by not reflecting?

PART VI

COACHING THROUGH THE HARD SPOTS

"Our most significant opportunities will be found in times of greatest difficulty."

—Thomas S. Monson

Most coaching tenures transpire on the heels of difficult times. That is to say, the person coming for coaching is often going through deep waters that seem impassable. During these times, a coach can come alongside and help. Coaching members of the emerging generation through the hard spots of life is a rewarding task for spiritual fathers and mothers.

Coaching under these circumstances requires utmost sensitivity and caution because rough spots are often God ordained as character-shaping events.[27] They can be the processing hand of God that indelibly prepares the person for what lies ahead. Remember, Jesus also was led by the Spirit into the wilderness to be tested.

In this section we will address tools that will equip you as a coach to provide skilled and excellent care for those you are preparing for life. But keep this in mind: coaching in the hard spots is not for the weak at heart.

38

CHISELING GOD'S MASTERPIECES

The Need for Human Interaction to Produce Real Change

"If you aren't in over your head, how do you know how tall you are?"

—T.S. Eliot

As a child growing up in the Ozark hills of Missouri, Branson was one of my favorite places to visit. I particularly enjoyed the theme park called Silver Dollar City.[28] Many of you have been there and know all about it. To visit SDC was to take a trip back in time to the 1800s. A day at the theme park was a treasure that offered itself annually for my family and me. Among the many experiences I embraced while there, none stands out more than a trip to the blacksmith shop.

Shad Heller was the old blacksmith who kept us entertained. He had an hourly show during which he demonstrated the art by creating everything from wagon wheels to horseshoes. I still remember his long, flowing beard, big glasses and the smell of smelting steel as he shaped the raw material into something useful and precious. Sparks would fly with every blow of his hammer; periodically, he would press the billows with his foot, heating the coals as he worked on his project. His craft could be summed up as "one who worked with raw iron."

In Bible days, especially the early days of ancient Israel, the work of the blacksmith was indispensable. It was imperative for the survival of the nations, peoples, and individuals. Their expertise affected everything from agriculture to national defense. They crafted tools, including axes, picks, plows, spades, hoes, and many other agricultural implements; arms, such as spears, multiple hand weapons, and war machinery; and many other needed items.

The days of blacksmithing (working with raw iron ore) are long gone for the most part; however, the concept still lingers. Oh, how we need individuals who can recognize potential in raw human material. We need men and women who can craft an unrefined generation and turn them into useful men and women of God. That is why I am so passionate about coaching. I believe the art of coaching can do just that.

A skilled coach has eyes to see that which is yet vague in the eyes of the person being coached. He spots in the raw material potential that is still unknown and undiscovered to others. The coach is like a blacksmith, taking what the person has his gifts, temperament, and callings and, in cooperation with the Holy Spirit, forms it into that which is yet to be; taking God-given potential and maximizing it to the fullest.

The Scriptures are full of examples. For instance, Jethro saw potential in Moses; Moses saw it in Joshua; Elijah recognized it in Elisha. Not surprisingly, the thread continues into the New Testament where Jesus saw God's hand working with the 12 apostles; Barnabas latched on to Paul; and Paul coached Timothy. So on down through history we see a great list of saints unleashing the potential in others.

Coaching has come of age. As spiritual fathers, we, in a small way, are helping chisel God's masterpieces. Have you learned to see potential in others? Are you skilled in working with raw material?

39

MINING THE METAL

How to Work With Raw Material

"Being challenged
in life is inevitable,
being defeated is optional."
—Roger Crawford

Raw material represents unrefined, un-tempered, imperfect people. Unfortunately, God-given potential rarely shows up in its purest form. Rather, it must be mined, refined, and purified. Then, and only then, is it ready for use.

Such is the case with the individuals you are coaching. They come to you in the form of raw material, making our coaching role similar to a treasure hunt. The potential must be spotted, brought to the surface, and developed. Only then can it become harnessed and made useful.

I have observed, however, that many people prefer working with a "finished product" rather than with the raw material. It is cleaner, less messy, and much more pliable. But someone must go after the unrefined potential. Will it be you? We must guard against the tendency of refusing to work with raw material, for the greatest possibilities often lie hidden within the iron ore of the human heart. It's our job to excavate it. As a matter of fact, most of the Bible's greatest leaders were formed from raw material. David best exhibits this process when he took a group of undesirables into the wilderness and turned them into an army of warriors and bodyguards (see 1 Chronicles 11:10-14).

Coaching for potential is hard work. It involves sorting through the impure metal of the human fabric and separating the good from the bad.

Three things to remember about capturing and developing the potential you see in your client:

1. It's a journey, not an event.

Try to rush the process and it usually short-circuits the plan.

2. It usually requires heat to shape the raw material.

Heat brings out all the impurities. What's in you, under pressure oozes out.

3. Once shaped, tempering is required.

Just because we're headed in the right direction doesn't mean the product is done.

Much more could be said about each of these however; we will look more closely at these three truths in succeeding chapters.

40
TURNING UP THE HEAT
Dealing With Issues in Others

"There is a tendency at every important but difficult crossroad to pretend that it's not really there."
—Bill McKibben

In yesteryears, the blacksmith's job included smelting the raw material to render it malleable. The reason for this process was twofold: (1) the product was impure in its natural state; and (2) It was rigid until heat was applied.

The same is true for the human heart.

This lesson can also be applied to the process of coaching for potential and is usually found to be a less than desirable procedure. Turning up the heat often takes both the coach and the client out of their comfort zones; nevertheless, it is necessary if God-given potential is to emerge.

As already stated, raw material rarely resembles the finished product. The process resembles the blacksmith's preparatory work. The metal must be heated to the melting point before it can be poured and shaped into a new form. It is the same material in substance; it is simply transformed into a new contour and purpose.

In much the same way, human lives are transformed by fire. The shaping of potential also requires heat, and this is the part of the process we dislike most. The pressures, challenges, and the difficult moments of life shape the human psyche and spirit in ways nothing else can do.

It is a necessary part of unleashing the potential within the person. In coaching, this procedure takes place when we help the person identify, name, and deal with constraints that impede their progress. A constraint is any habit, behavior, or thought process that hinders the person from being all God wants him to be.

The process just described is the way transformation takes place in a person. The end result in this metamorphosis is that God-given potential moves forward to become an assignment from God. But it all begins with heat.

41

IT IS A JOURNEY, NOT AN EVENT

Learning How To Persevere

"Sweat equity is the most valuable equity there is. Know your business and industry better than anyone else in the world. Love what you do or don't do it."

—Mark Cuban

Walking out your life purpose is anything but easy. It takes commitment to a life of being challenged and a willingness to be stretched and pulled in various directions. At times it can be confusing and totally frustrating. Is it any wonder so many pilgrims on the journey lose their way and return to their proverbial Egypt?

I like what my friend and leadership guru, Dr. Sam Chand says, "I propose that leaders can grow only to the level of their pain tolerance, no further." So what is the answer to attaining your God-given potential? It is found in understanding that the road to your God-given potential is a journey, not an event. Pain, if tolerated, means gain.

The following principles will help you coach those walking through this valley:

1. View life with perspective.

We must all learn that it is impossible see around life's corners. You are not the only one with things going on that are beyond your comprehension. It is okay not to have the answers.

2. Do not view life strictly from a linear perspective.

As Westerners, we often develop the mindset that things have to happen in a linear progression: this one thing has to happen in order for the next to transpire. Interestingly, the Hebraic mind views life as cyclical. In other words, you may not be able to connect the dots now, but somewhere in the future, purpose and meaning emerge. Perspective is important.

3. Learn to cherish the moment that you might enjoy the journey.

As a friend of mine once said, "Never weigh yourself every day." I laughed because I understood the metaphor that simply meant, learn to enjoy where you are today. Enjoy the journey more than the one event.

Jesus put it this way: "Do not worry about tomorrow, for tomorrow will worry about itself" (Matthew 6:34). To enjoy the moment is to savor the journey.

Remember, it's a journey, not an event!

42

TAKING THE LONG WAY HOME

The Will of God Moves Slower Than You Think It Should

"If I could store any character quality in a cookie jar, I'd store patience. Chocolate-chip patience cookies. And I'd eat them all at one sitting."

—Jarod Kintz

I am a Steven Curtis Chapman fan. I have been listening to his music for many years. In fact, I like nearly everything he sings. In a recent release titled, "The Long Way Home," he addresses the valleys, challenges, and battles in his pilgrim journey. Can anybody relate?

As explained in an earlier chapter, I have learned that God rarely operates on our timetable. If you don't believe me, ask anyone who has walked with God for any length of time. The thought of God being in a hurry is ludicrous. As my grandma used to say, "It just 'ain't' so."

If this is fact and it is then the combined traits of biblical patience and flexibility are great virtues. According to Scripture, patience is required if we hope to inherit the promises of God. Do you have those biblical qualities? (See Hebrews 6:10.)

The realization of one's God-given potential takes time. That comprehension moves at various paces, depending primarily on two key factors: (1) the person's specific season of life; and (2) his level of desire and passion to move forward. As a coach, you must consider these variables in your pursuit of potential.

Concerning the first variable, if you can help your client gain insight into the specific season he is currently navigating, then the span of time becomes less of an issue. In regards to the second variable, spiritual desire is easy to lose. It can be substituted easily with other passions causing the person to not even realize it is missing. Coaching that centers on these issues can be beneficial and productive.

Knowing that God's work in us is never accomplished overnight is a powerful realization. By the same token, knowing oneself is never an overnight development. God is so awesome that He can't be known all at once. And since you and your client are fearfully and wonderfully made and His purposes for your lives are so marvelous, they cannot be grasped immediately.

Yes, God's will often moves slower than we think it should. So, it is I (and you) who must slow down and walk out His plan with patience and endurance.

43

ENGAGING THE ISSUES AT HAND

Knowing How and When To Confront

"What are you accepting
that would not be a part
of your ideal day?"

—Alan Cohen

Addressing an inhibiting issue in the person you are coaching is never easy. In fact, it can be a prickly situation for both you and your client. An inhibiting issue would be anything that is holding him back or constraining him from reaching his God-given potential. From time to time in your coaching experience you have to engage these types of topics.

So what is the secret to engaging ugly issues? How do I initiate the process? When is the right time? Is there a right time? Answering these and other questions is important, if problems are to be solved in a proper manner.

I have found that engaging an issue always begins with an accurate assessment, both of the client and his understanding of the situation. The source of some hindrances can be traced to blind spots; therefore, we must never assume that the client even sees the issue.

The following list of suggestions is designed to help you assess where your client's situation regarding the issues you feel need to be addressed.

1. Discover the client's sense of awareness regarding the issue.

As a coach, make no assumptions; the individual may be part of the problem and not even realize it.

The best test for determining awareness is to ask what I call "ownership questions." These queries force a client to review his role in the problem and how it affects the other party. For instance: "What is your role in this current dilemma, and how might it be affecting the situation?" By asking one simple question, you may begin to assess the client's awareness of his or her role in the problem.

2. Look for a sense of responsibility, or lack of responsibility, regarding the issue.

If the person has a clear understanding of how his behavior or attitude is affecting the situation, you will know immediately how to proceed. Pride or self-preservation is usually hiding in the mix as the client plays the blame game. So after carefully assessing the problem, you will be able to decide the next move.

If the issue is a blind spot in the person, consider taking an indirect approach without harshness (a backdoor approach, if you will). If the situation concerns a lack of responsibility, try assuming a direct, hard-hitting position.

Engaging impeding matters is never fun, but as a coach you must periodically press the issue.

44

WOULD YOU HOLD ME ACCOUNTABLE?

Understanding Healthy Accountability

"Change before you have to."

—Jack Welch

The word *accountability* is defined as "the state of being accountable, liable, or answerable. It's the act of making yourself answerable to another individual in a certain area(s) of one's life."[29]

Accountability is extremely important in the coaching field because change is never easy. So how do I hold a client accountable? How do I press the issue when inconsistencies appear? Here are three steps I take in helping a person take responsibility for his life.

1. Secure permission to deal with an accountability issue.

Most people don't realize that accountability is always a voluntary issue. It is never a matter of coercion. In other words, you can't hold someone accountable unless he wants you to do so. You can enforce a judgment or rule...but get the person to submit? I don't think so. He may lie, dodge the issue, recuse himself and play the avoidance game.

Gaining permission is crucial. It disarms perceived threats that come with accountability issues. Obtaining consent helps the client recognize your help as an intervention from God. When this step is ignored, your help may be perceived as an intrusion that violates the individual's personal and private life.

2. Endeavor not to use "why" questions when dealing with accountability issues.

"Why questions tend to put people in a defensive mode. They may feel as though they are being interrogated, forced to defend themselves, and asked to justify themselves. Instead of asking the "why" questions, ask "what" and "how" questions instead (see example below).

3. Learn to ask good, open-ended questions.

As described in an earlier chapter, open-ended questions require more than a one-word answer, particularly "yes" or "no." Open-ended questions force the person to go inside, to process the issue. These types of questions also tend to broaden the conversation rather than narrowing it.

Here's is a brief example of an accountability conversation:

Coach: "Is it okay if we talk about the issue of _____ (fill in the blank)? (This is the permission phase.)

Coach: "Tell me what is keeping you from _____ (fill in the blank)." (This is the avoidance of the "why" question.)

"What do you need to do to keep from _____ (fill in the blank)?"

Notice how these open-ended questions require the client to process and reflect on the topic.

Accountability is vital in helping our clients to unleash their God-given potential. Do you know how to make it work for you and the person you are coaching?

45

STRETCHING THE MOLD

Creating a Mental Image Using Metaphors

"Disneyland will never
be completed. It will continue
to grow as long as there is
imagination left in the world."

—Walt Disney

Intentional cognitive exercise is a valuable tool in helping your client discover and unleash his God-given potential. It will become necessary at times to stretch the client's mind beyond his normal level of thought, to help him think in new paradigms.

The idea of cognitive exercise does not refer to solving crossword puzzles or playing Sudoku. Rather, it relates to helping the client create mental metaphors of his own experience and story.

Most Westerners are not accustomed to using metaphors in everyday speech; however, Jesus was a master at it. He reminded Peter that he was a rock (Petros, Matthew 16:18). He called Herod a fox, the Pharisees white-walled tombs, and made many similar comparisons using metaphorical language.

By now you are probably wondering, *Where do I start? How do I do this?* Here are a few tips that should help:

1. Encourage the client find a metaphor that suits who he is as a person.

The human mind has the ability to think in pictures. When I say, "red barn," the mind automatically pictures a red barn. Actually, a specific area of the brain was designed for this very purpose. Because of our western paradigm of thinking, this part of the brain is severely lacking in stimulation. Thinking metaphorically literally engages that part of the brain and unleashes its creativity.

2. Encourage the client to find a metaphor that best describes his challenge.

The use of metaphorical language causes the client to think in more concrete terms and allows the creative part of the brain to become active.

Helping the client think metaphorically gets the ball rolling so he is able to "process" the issue. It launches a fresh way of seeing the issue, which, in turn, leads to progress. Here is how you might initiate the conversation with the person you are coaching: "Using the metaphor of a garden, describe what is happening in the garden of your life at this season."

Andrew Ortony, a Stanford University researcher in learning and cognition made a radical statement some years ago: "Metaphors are necessary, not just nice."[30] He went on to show that using metaphors create powerful, rapid learning by linking what is unfamiliar or novel with what the person already knows.

The human mind is capable of grasping many powerful metaphors, including the following examples:

• Games

- Garden
- Journey or trip
- Seasons
- Sports
- Weather
- Books
- A road or path

I know it's a strange concept, but Jesus frequently spoke in metaphors. Solomon used them to pen the Proverbs. Modern poets and musicians use them regularly, and even modern technology gets in on it (Apple Computers the Cloud).

Why can't we use them? We can! Go ahead and try it, it could be life changing.

PART VII

VARIOUS AND SUNDRY ITEMS OF IMPORTANCE

"Deep in the human subconscious is a pervasive need for a logical universe that makes sense. But the real universe is always one step beyond logic."

—Frank Herbert

This final section discusses a variety of issues that surface periodically when one is coaching the next generation. Although the content of this division may seem scattered, it includes a good representation of what you will experience when coaching your spiritual sons and daughters.

In the process of coaching, you will find yourself tracking in one area, when, suddenly, you discover that adjustments need to be made. Making those changes is crucial in order to move toward the help the person needs.

Various unforeseen items will arise!

46

LIVE SO NOTHING IS WASTED

Gleaning From the Clues God Has Left In Your Life

"It is strange that people train themselves so carefully to go to waste so prematurely."

—Robert Aickman

Thirty years is a long time, but it happens to be the number of years I have been in ministry. As you can see, I started early. I was converted at age nineteen, and by the time I was twenty-two, I had preached my first message. It seems like only yesterday.

So what's all the hoopla about thirty? Well, I suppose there is nothing really special about the number, other than the fact that recently I sensed the Lord challenging me to prepare myself for the next thirty years of ministry.

I'm not brash enough to assume that my recent encounter with God is to be taken as a promise for thirty more years although it could be! However, I did sense that God was challenging me to look back and reminisce on my life in order to distill valuable principles that can be passed on to fellow travelers. It was as if the Lord was saying to me, "Do not let anything in your life be wasted!"

In much the same way, those you are coaching need to learn to revisit life's moving experiences and glean from them valuable lessons and principles. We live in a fast-paced society that has a tendency to overlook important lessons that can be learned only from life itself.

The book of Proverbs teaches us that wisdom calls out in the streets. It speaks to us in everyday situations we encounter. Hidden within your client's experiences lie many pieces to the puzzle we call potential. The key to learning from these occurrences is to revisit them systematically.

Here's how I have my clients start. We begin by noting what I call "emotionally moving experiences." It could be something that happened 20 years ago, or an encounter as recent as yesterday. Within these seemingly "coincidental happenings" is a wealth of wisdom and knowledge, if they can be unpacked in a biblical manner.

Next, I ask the client to journal the experience and unpack feelings, emotions, and his intuitions concerning them. Details are important; emotions have meaning. Why? Because brain science is now showing us that all learning is tied to an emotion, either negative or positive. In other words, both negative and positive experiences have the ability to bestow wisdom.

Finally, I ask the person I am coaching to record what he senses God is (or was) saying to him in the middle of the situation. If he is unsure, I simply have him record what he *thinks* God might have been saying.

From here, we visit those places together to glean valuable information that helps the client discover his God-given potential.

47

COMING OUT OF YOUR SHELL—PART I

How To Coach Introverts

"Introverts keep their best stuff inside—that is, until it is ready. And this drives extroverts crazy!"

—Laurie Helgoe

According to recent studies by social experts, "extroversion" is now deemed to be a necessary trait if one hopes to gain cultural acceptance. Marti Olsen Laney, psychologist and author of the book, *The Introvert Advantage,* says, "We live in a culture that caters to and extols extroverts. We definitely learn that extroversion is the way we should be."[31] Jonathan Rauch, writer for *The Atlantic,* stated that introverts are "among the most misunderstood and aggrieved groups in America, possibly the world."[32]

Not only has this assumption filled American culture, it has, in many ways, infiltrated the church and various religious groups. In his book, *Introverts in the Church,* Adam McHugh describes how professors at a Christian college asked students to rate the person of Jesus Christ according to the profiles of temperament found in the Briggs-Meyers Type Indicator. The study revealed that 97 percent of the students rated Him as an extrovert.[33]

A reasonable question would be: "Where does this kind of cultural bent and attitude place the average introverted leader?" The answer is simple; it leaves many of them feeling as though they are intellectually inferior or perhaps with a sense of incompetence and inadequacy. Depending on a person's level of maturity, this can be debilitating and extremely frustrating.

You may be wondering what this has to do with helping people unleash their potential. In order to help your client better understand himself, you must show him how to navigate the extrovert and introvert biases, since they can affect the way he processes and moves through life.

Here are a few realities to keep in mind:

1. No one is totally extroverted or introverted.

It is comforting to know that every individual has the ability to operate in both realms; however, everyone leans toward one characteristic or the other. For example, even though I am primarily an introvert, I can be extremely sociable and outgoing with some groups and in certain situations.

2. The way we reenergize emotionally is what differentiates us.

The introvert recharges primarily by withdrawing from social interaction. This doesn't mean he is shy or lacking social skills, it just means he is an inward person and needs "alone time" to recoup. The extrovert, on the other hand, is reenergized by social interaction. Alone time drives an extrovert "up the wall."

Pay attention to how the person you are coaching reenergizes, and you will be able to know if he is an "innie" or an "outie."

3. Introverts need time to process; extroverts process spontaneously.

Because of their natural tendency of needing time to process life, introverts can seem aloof or withdrawn. But, if you can honor this characteristic in their life, they can be quite productive in meetings and social gatherings.

Extroverts process life on the go, usually as they speak and do. That is why they are often thought of as being quick witted and verbal.

So to get an introvert out of his shell, you must understand these things and give him time to work. For instance, if you send an introvert coworker the agenda for your board meeting ahead of time, you'll likely receive more vocal participation from him. He doesn't do well with, "Can you have this job done in one hour?"

Know the individual character traits of the people you are coaching. It will help both them and you. Ask yourself, "Am I coaching an 'innie' or an 'outie'?"

48

COMING OUT OF YOUR SHELL-PART II

I'm an Introvert and Proud of It

"Introverts may have strong social skills and enjoy parties and business meetings, but after a while wish they were home in their pajamas..."

—Susan Cain

Attention all introverts: you are a different breed, and it's time to accept and celebrate your uniqueness! According to Dr. Marti Olsen Laney, author of *The Introvert Advantage*, our uniqueness centers around three main traits that earmark us for introversion: (1) The way you recharge your emotional batteries; (2) The way you respond to outside stimulation; and (3) Your need for depth rather than breadth.[34]

With that said, I have compiled a list of statements from Laney's book that I hope will broaden our understanding with regard to the three traits that make us unique. Borrowing from her words, I have rephrased these remarks in first person plural to accentuate them and make a point. If you consider yourself an introvert, examine these statements carefully and you will see yourself. If you are extroverted, perhaps you will catch a new glimpse of your introverted friend, boss, or spouse.

- We are different as introverts, but we don't need to apologize for it.
- We love social relationships, but they drain us emotionally.
- Because of the draining effect of social interaction on our emotional energy, we tend to avoid extended sessions with large crowds.
- In light of the above, we don't need a large number of relationships, just meaningful and real ones.
- We don't mean to come across aloof and mysterious, we are by nature more private and thus reveal less of ourselves to the average person.
- We keep a lot of our energy inside, often making it difficult for others to know us.
- Because of our deeply reflective nature, we tend to hesitate before we speak.
- Like it or not, we are usually absorbed in thought, processing life from the inside out.
- We usually proceed with caution in most matters.
- Right or wrong, we usually don't offer our ideas freely; we generally need to be asked.
- If you try to analyze us by viewing our body language, you will not get an accurate reading. We are not as expressive or demonstrative as our counterparts.
- Unfortunately, our facial expressions do not always tell the whole story. We need to work on this!
- We are usually hesitant to engage extroverts we do not know well...and some we do!
- When we speak, we generally have something to say.

- We do not necessarily desire more conversation, just deeper ones.
- The same goes for our relationships, life experiences, information, and almost every other area of our lives.
- We tend to over stimulate easily. Rapid amounts of information, excitement, emotion, conversation, etc., and our minds go...TILT. Remember, we internalize and process *everything*.
- There is much more about us you need to know and we need to tell.

The above statements broaden the three main traits that make us introverted. Are you coaching an introverted leader? If so, you will need to work with him, simply because they tend to move at a slower pace. You might even get a few more "I don't know" answers. That is normal.

49

COMING OUT OF YOUR SHELL-PART III

Tips for Coaching the Introverted Client

"Where in your life did you become uncomfortable with the sweet territory of silence?"

—Native American saying

Coaching introverts can be a challenging endeavor because they are often difficult to read and generally unemotional and non-verbal.

In view of these facts, I suggest that you take the following course of action. Be sure to engage each of these steps at some time during the coaching experience.

1. Celebrate the fact that your introverted client is created different.

In a world in which extroverts outnumber introverts three to one, remember that as an "innie" he is not second rate or a misfit. He is God's creation.

2. Encourage the introvert to nurture his extroverted side.

Coax him to venture out of his "innie" world and learn to do a few things as an "outie." Require him to tolerate the strange new feeling of not quite being himself.

3. Teach him to gain more self-awareness concerning how he reenergizes.

An "innie" will turn inward to reenergize. Encourage him to define what he really likes to do. Is it reading? Is it enjoying an activity with a spouse? Perhaps it is prayer, contemplation, or something as simple as tinkering. Teach him to observe himself.

4. Suggest that he take more short breaks during the day.

Encourage him to break out of the old routine periodically every day. Take a short walk or step outside; as Rick Warren says, "Divert daily."

5. Help him take note of what seems to drain his emotional energy.

Instruct the person you are coaching to prepare beforehand when he knows heavy social interaction lies ahead. To be fore-warned is to be prepared.

6. Support him in nurturing his spiritual life.

As a rule an introvert is inclined to seek deep spiritual meaning. If he is not satisfying that need through his walk with Christ, a void will always be present.

7. Encourage the introvert to base his confidence on who he is rather than on what he does.

This is so important because many of the introverts' skills, talents, and abilities are devalued in an extroverted world.

Coaching introverts can seem a little more laborious than coaching extraverts. You must learn how they think and how to pull their thoughts out of them. Timing is critical; they cannot be rushed or they will shut down. Keep in mind that inside the introvert is a treasure you can develop. It's worth the challenge.

50

REFRAMING FAILURE

Giving Yourself Permission to Take Risks

"It's never too late to become what you might have been."

—George Elliot

I was embarrassed! I had just sat through an entire meeting grossly misunderstanding the agenda. It finally dawned on me: I was on a different page than everyone else. I had even made a few ignorant comments. Much to my dismay, I hadn't thoroughly read the memo. Fortunately, only a handful of people were present.

As I left the meeting, I felt about two inches tall; know what I mean? Later, while seated at my desk, I felt the Lord nudge me, encouraging me to make this slip-up a learning experience. So I grabbed my pen and jotted down the specific lessons I needed to learn from this real-life blunder.

These points have become a tool I have used often to help clients reframe failure. What did I learn? Basically, that tremendous power can be found in "unpacking a failure." Here are a few tips on how to analyze failure with the person you are coaching:

1. Take time to revisit the disappointing experience.

All failures contain information, powerful clues that can translate into lessons learned. Take time to jot down what you saw and how you felt. Pull aside for a few minutes and recapture the feeling, then record the emotion of the moment. Review it while it's still fresh.

2. Journal what you learned from the incident.

Each of us must choose to ignore the nagging voice of failure in order to make the blunder a learning experience. Accept it for what it is...then move on. Ask yourself, "What lessons did I learn?" Remember, valuable lessons are waiting to be gleaned from all failures.

3. Talk your client through what he might do next time in a similar situation.

It is a good idea to list those things you *would not* do next time along with the things you *will* do! I did that several years ago following a lengthy building program during my pastoral days. I still have the list; it would be helpful advice for those pastors engaged in building programs.

4. Walk your client through the question, "What is God saying to me through this failure?"

It is also important to ask, "Did you recognize God in the situation?" Remember, I sensed God nudging me and admonishing me to move on to make my blunder a learning experience. Have the client write down what he feels God is saying to him, even if he isn't sure. The pen helps clarify what the mind is pondering.

Analyzing a failure can be a painful process; however, many principles can be learned from these incidences in our lives. Think about Jesus' experience: the writer to the Hebrews says, "Although he was a son, he learned obedience from what he suffered." (Hebrews 5:8) What are some things you have learned by unpacking a failure?

51

UNHURRIED TIME

Taking Time To Grow

"How did it get so late so soon?"
—Dr. Seuss

I recently came across a new term that impacted my life in a positive way. The thought came from noted author and minister, Henry Blackaby. He was being interviewed and used the phrase, "unhurried time," in reference to a leader's devotional life.[35] His statement was that every leader must learn to work unhurried time into his schedule.

That thought challenged and even convicted me about my own life. Unhurried time is a must for anyone seeking to discover and unleash his God-given potential. As life coaches, it is imperative that we impress upon the hearts and minds of our clients the importance of unhurried time. The concept hinges on the fact that we must slow down to "see life." How about you? How long has it been since you have taken a little "unhurried time" with God?

Here are a few thoughts about unhurried time (UT) and how to create and preserve it.

1. UT clears your mind and heart to attend solely to God.

Most of us simply glance in God's general direction periodically rather than waiting for Him with anticipation and longing. We have the Martha syndrome; we are encumbered with much serving (see Luke 10:41).

2. UT fosters intimacy with God.

Unhurried time leads to our becoming acquainted with God's heart tugs. His impressions are clearer, resulting in greater affection for Him and His values.

3. UT allows us to listen more clearly.

As we listen more carefully, we understand more deeply.

We all suffer from "hurried sickness" from time to time. If we are not careful, hurrying can become a way of life, even when it is not necessary.

52

LEARNING THE SPIRITUAL COACHING STANCE

What Works Best in Today's Culture and Why

"I don't imagine you will dispute the fact that at present the stupid people are in an absolutely overwhelming majority all the world over."

—Henrik Ibsen

Why would *I* need a coach?

I hear that question periodically as I share the coaching movement around the country. In a world filled with millions of books and endless resources and sources of information at my fingertips...*me,* need a coach? I can just Google or Bing it, can't I?

Although some of these responses have some validity, the primary reason people need a life coach is because information and knowledge alone cannot change lives. Life transformation requires human interaction.

So what is coaching? Simply put, coaching is the art of coming alongside a leader and facilitating his growth. A coach is a change agent who helps leaders take responsibility for and maximize their own God-given potential.

Would-be coaches face three common challenges:

1. The shift from telling to asking.

Coaches are not so much tellers as they are askers. Their role is not to fix people but to help them think in new and fresh paradigms. A true coach leads his clients on a journey of discovery of truth.

It has been said that a coach is a cross between a cheering section and a nagging mother!

2. The shift from doing all the thinking to allowing the person being coached to think for himself.

The coach does not view himself as the expert, even when he might have the upper hand in experience and knowledge. Rather, a good coach sees himself as a change catalyst. His primary goal is to help his client have an "ah ha" moment—a flash of insight.

He knows the greatest motivational factor for adults is not being told every step to make, but rather the moment of self-awareness or God-awareness.

3. The difficult shift from no faith in people to being confident in them.

It is paradoxical to believe in the depravity of mankind on one hand and to acknowledge on the other that he is created in the image of God. Yet it seems these ironies coexist. (No I am not being heretical. Yes, I believe depraved man cannot find his own way to God.)

Have you ever considered the fact that God handed over the earth to mankind, knowing he would fail? And have you wondered why Jesus left the planet and His work in the hands of eleven men who a short time earlier had denied Him? I probably would not have done that. Could our lack of confidence in people set them up to fail? Possibly.

Coaching is a new paradigm, an innovative tool that meets the culture where it is and opens the door for truth. Who needs coaching? My question is, "Who doesn't?" I believe the culture is ripe for coaching. Who's ready to begin?

Conclusion
MY FINAL
{Kuhn-kloo'-zuhn}

"You never change things by fighting the existing reality. To change something, build a new model that makes the existing model obsolete."
—Richard Buckminster

An ancient writer once described the certitude of change by stating, "The only constant in life, is *change* itself."

In an age of rapid change and shifting learning models, could it be that the church itself desperately needs a more fitting model through which she can fulfill the Great Commission of discipling the nations? Could it be that our discipleship model and method has become outdated and ineffective, leaving us barren and unfruitful in the task at hand? I for one think so.

As we study church history we will discover that people in different epochs of time have gravitated toward diverse methods of discipleship. However, most models have remained *relationally* oriented. For instance, the first century church primarily discipled through the *small group* model known as house churches. The church under Constantine and Rome primarily used an *experience* model based on the use of gothic cathedrals, icons, and mass, etc. Under Martin Luther and the Reformation believer's discipleship morphed into an *academic model,* or more of an intellectual approach. The point is twofold; 1) Although the models changed, they remained *relationally* oriented. 2) The church must continue her periodic adjustment of discipleship to fit the culture and era of the generation it is called to reach.

Today's church is more adept as an "academic model" of discipleship, one that resembles the Reformation model, however with a few subtle shifts. The primary shift reflects a modified model that embraces the notion that "mere information" is transformational. Of course this is a reflection of our cultural shift into the Information Age and the idea that information is power. Information-based discipleship says, "just read a book, take a test, or sit through a class, and you are now a disciple." Nothing could be further from the truth. I believe information can inspire and is absolutely necessary, however the Jesus model of discipleship touts the fact that human interaction is a must for real life change. It says, "You really don't know something until you experience it, and it's the human interaction that helps you process the experience." Coaching fits this paradigm.

Thankfully there are various emerging methods of discipleship through which the Great Commission may perhaps be more effectively carried out. I believe the model displayed in this book (*discipleship coaching*) could very well be one of the contemporary models that will affect today's generation in a positive and powerful way.

Hopefully you are beginning to catch a glimpse of the new paradigm that I believe must evolve in order to move us closer to fulfilling the Great Commission. Outdated and non-biblical discipleship and leadership philosophies must begin to shift. New, more biblical methodologies must be embraced.

In *kuhn **kloo** zuhn*, I believe we cannot deny the fact that Jesus' main method of discipleship and leadership development was the *coaching* model. He practiced it regularly. It was a Hebraic model of relational learning, coupled with teaching that stemmed from real life experiences, rooted in the Torah and prophets. His answers often came in the form of powerful questions; He broke through barriers by being authentic rather than using His positional authority. He simply modeled that which He wanted His followers to discover. We must do the same.

Will the church embrace this silent revolution that we aptly call *coaching?* Only time will tell. So are you ready to roll up your sleeves and start *Unleashing God-given Potential?* To start, *"...Coaching the Next Generation?"* I hope you are.

As alluded to in a previous chapter, I think my last question would be, "Who needs coaching anyway? *...My* response, *"Who doesn't?"*

Notes

Introduction

[1] Gary Collins, PHD, *Christian Coaching, Helping Others Turn Potential into Reality,* NavPress, Colorado Springs, Colorado, 2009.

[2] Wayne Gretsky, http://en.wikipedia.org/wiki/Wayne_Gretzky, Accessed 6/19/12.

Chapter 1

[3] Rick Warren, *The Purpose Drive Life,* Zondervan, Grand Rapids, Michigan, 2003, p. 11.

Chapter 3

[4] http://dictionary.reference.com/browse/destiny?s=t, accessed 6/18/12.

Chapter 4

[5] J. Robert Clinton, *Strategic Concepts That Clarify a Focused Life,* Barnabas Publishers, Altadena, California, 2005.

Chapter 5

[6] F.F. Bruce, *The Book of Acts,* Grand Rapids, Michigan, William B. Eerdmans Publishing Co., 1988, p. 101.

[7] Arrington French, *The Book of Acts,* Hendrickson Publishers, Peabody, New York, 1988, p. 53.

Chapter 6

[8] Holy Bible, *Amplified Version,* Zondervan and Lockyer Foundation, 1987.

Chapter 8

[9] Susan Scott, *Fierce Conversations,* Berkley Publishing Group, New York, New York, 2002. p. 118.

[10] Scott, p. 91.

Chapter 10

[11] J. Robert Clinton, "Mentoring," class notes from GLEAD 5303 Spiritual Formation of a Leader, Southwestern Christian University, Sept. 2003.

[12] Clinton, class notes.

Chapter 12

[13] http://dictionary.reference.com/browse/catalyze?s=t, accessed 6/12/12.

Chapter 14

[14] Adapted from *Implementation Module,* by Tony Stoltzfus & D. Lyn Eichmann, LifeForming Coaching, Virginia Beach Virginia, 2008, IR-4.

Chapter 15

[15] Stoltzfus & Eichmann, IR-4.

Chapter 17

[16] Elisabeth Engelberg and Lennart Sjöberg, *CyberPsychology & Behavior,* February 2004, 7(1): 41-47. doi:10.1089/10949310-4322820101.

Chapter 18

[17] Margret J. Wheatley, *Turning To One Another,* Berrett-Koehler Publishers, Inc., San Francisco, California, 2002, p. 5.

[18] Patrick Williams and Diane S. Menendez, *Becoming a Professional Life Coach,* W.W. Norton & Company, New York, New York, 2007.

Chapter 21

[19] Susan Scott, *Fierce Conversations,* Berkley Publishing Group, New York, New York, 2002, p. 13.

Chapter 22

[20] Tony Stoltzfus & D. Lyn Eichmann, *Formation Training Module*, LifeForming Leadership Coaching, Virginia Beach, Virginia, 2009, IR-9.

Chapter 25

[21] Patrick Williams and Diane S. Menendez, *Becoming a Professional Life Coach*, W.W. Norton & Company, New York, New York, 2007, p. 22.

[22] Tony Stoltzfus & D. Lyn Eichmann, *ACT Manual*, LifeForming Leadership Coaching, Virginia Beach, Virginia, p. 57.

Chapter 26

[23] Tony Stoltzfus & D. Lyn Eichmann, *Implementation Module Manual*, LifeForming Leadership Coaching, Virginia Beach, Virginia, IR-8.

Chapter 27

[24] NCIS, *National Broadcasting Company* (NBC), New York, New York, 2012.

Chapter 32

[25] Tony Stoltzfus & D. Lyn Eichmann, *Implementation Module Manual*, LifeForming Leadership Coaching, Virginia Beach, Virginia, IR-9.

Chapter 34

[26] Daniel Goleman, Richard Boyatzis, Annie McKee, *Primal Leadership, Realizing the power of Emotional Intelligence*, Boston, Harvard Business School Press, 2002, p.30

Part VI

[27] J. Robert Clinton uses this terminology when referring to God's hand of change and tempering in our life.

Chapter 38

[28] Silver Dollar City, Branson Mo, is a theme park nestled in the Ozark Mountains of Missouri.

Chapter 44

[29] http://dictionary.reference.com/browse/accountability?s=t, accessed 6/19/12.

Chapter 45

[30] Anthony Ortony, *Educational Theory*, 45-53, reprinted from *Becoming a Professional Life Coach*, W.W. Norton & Co., New York, New York, 2007, p. 132.

Chapter 47

[31] Marti Olsen Laney, *The Introvert Advantage*, Workman Publishing Co. Inc., New York, New York, 2002. Mrs. Laney is a great contributor to the study of introversion in today's culture. For her credit, most of my thoughts and concepts are borrowed from her ideas in the above mentioned book.

[32] Jonathan Rauch, http://www.theatlantic.com/magazine/archive/2003/03/caring-for-your-introvert/2696/, accessed 6/12/12.

[33] Adam S. McHugh, *Introverts in the Church, Finding Our Place in an Extroverted Culture*, InterVarsity Press, Downers Grove, Illinois, 2009.

Chapter 48

[34] Marti Olsen Laney, *The Introvert Advantage*, Workman Publishing Co. Inc., New York, New York, 2002.

Chapter 51

[35] Henry Blackaby and Richard Blackaby, *Spiritual Leadership*, Broadman & Holman Publishers, Nashville Tennessee, 2001, p. 212.

Bibliography

Blackaby Henry, and Blackaby Richard. *Spiritual Leadership.* Tennessee: Broadman & Holman Publishers, 2001.

Bruce, F.F. *The Book of Acts.* Grand Rapids: Eerdmans Publishing Co., 1988.

Clinton, J. Robert. *Connecting.* Altadena: Barnabas Publishers, 1992.

———, *Strategic Concepts That Clarify a Focused Life.* Altadena: Barnabas Publishers, 1995.

Collins, Gary. *Christian Coaching: Helping Others Turn Potential into Reality.* NavPress: Colorado Springs, 2009.

Arrington, French. *The Book of Acts.* Peabody, New York: Hendrickson Publishers, 1988.

Goleman, Daniel. *Emotional Intelligence: Why It Can Matter More Than IQ.* Bloomsburg: Bloomsbury, 2010.

Holy Bible, Amplified Version, Zondervan and Lockyer Foundation, 1987.

Laney, Marti Olsen. *The Introvert Advantage.* New York: Workman Publishing Co, 2002.

McHugh, Adam S. *Introverts in the Church: Finding Our Place in an Extroverted Culture.* Downers Grove: Inter-Varsity Press, 2009.

NCIS, National Broadcasting Company (NBC), New York, NY, 2012.

Anthony, Ortony, *Educational Theory,* 45-53, reprinted from Becoming a Professional Life Coach, W.W. Norton & Co., New York, New York, 2007.

Scott, Susan. *Fierce Conversations.* New York: Berkley Publishing Group, 2002.

Stoltzfus, Tony and Eichmann, Lyn D. *Implementation Module.* Virginia Beach: LifeForming Coaching, 2008.

Stoltzfus, Tony and Eichmann, Lyn D. *ACT Manual.* Virginia Beach: LifeForming Leadership Coaching, 2008

Warren, Rick. *The Purpose Drive Life.* Grand Rapids, Michigan: Zondervan, 2003.

Wheatley, Margret J. *Turning To One Another.* San Francisco, California: Berrett-Koehler Publishers, 2002.

Williams, Patrick, and Menendez, Dianne S. *Becoming a Professional Life Coach.* New York: W.W. Norton & Company, 2007.

Online Sources:

Engelberg, Elisabeth, and Sjöberg, Lennart. *CyberPsychology & Behavior,* 7(1): 41-47. doi:10.1089/109493104322820101 (accessed February 2004).

Wayne, Gretsky, http://en.wikipedia.org/wiki/Wayne_Gretzky. (accessed June 15, 2012)

Jonathan Rauch, http://www.theatlantic.com/magazine/archive/2003/03/caring-for-your-introvert/2696. (accessed April 15, 2012).

Tony Schwartz, "The Magic of Doing One Thing at a Time," *Harvard Business Review,* http://blogs.hbr.org/schwartz/2012/03/the-magic-of-doing-one-thing-a.html?referral=00563&cm_mmc=email-_-newsletter-_-daily_alert-_-alert_date&utm_source=newsletter_daily_alert&utm_medium=email&utm_campaign=alert_date. (accessed May 23, 2012).

http://dictionary.reference.com/browse/destiny?s=t.

http://goodreads.com/quotes. (accessed May1-June 23, 2012).

Author Contact Information

To purchase books, for more information, or to schedule John Chasteen to speak, please contact:

John Chasteen
Oklahoma City, OK
405-757-7740

john@heycoachjohn.com
www.heycoachjohn.com

Hey Coach John is an online training and community experience designed for both seasoned coaches, as well as those who are inquiring about coach training. At Hey Coach John, you will experience world-class training and interaction from one of today's most insightful coaches, John Chasteen. Coach John is a trainer of trainers and a leading authority when it comes to the Christian coaching movement.